FROM AGRICULTURE TO SERVICES

Volume 69, Sage Library of Social Research

Sage Library of Social Research

FROM AGRICULTURE TO SERVICES
The Transformation of Industrial Employment

Joachim Singelmann

Volume 69
SAGE LIBRARY OF
SOCIAL RESEARCH

 SAGE PUBLICATIONS   Beverly Hills   London

For information address:

SAGE PUBLICATIONS, INC.  SAGE PUBLICATIONS LTD
275 South Beverly Drive   28 Banner Street
Beverly Hills, California 90212   London EC1Y 8QE

Printed in the United States of America

Library of Congress Cataloging in Publication Data

Singelmann, Joachim.
    From agriculture to services: The Transformation of
    Industrial Employment
    (Sage library of social research; 69)
    Includes bibliographical references and index.
    1. Industrial sociology. 2. Service industries
workers. 3. Labor supply. I. Title.
HD6955.S57   301.5'5   78-19843
ISBN 0-8039-1092-4
ISBN 0-8039-1093-2 pbk.

FIRST PRINTING

CONTENTS

A WORKER READS HISTORY

Who built the seven gates of Thebes?
The books are filled with names of kings.
Was it kings who hauled the craggy blocks of stone?
And Babylon, so many times destroyed,
Who built the city up each time? In which of Lima's houses,
That city glittering with gold, lived those who built it?
In the evening when the Chinese wall was finished
Where did the masons go? Imperial Rome
Is full of arcs of triumph. Who reared them up? Over whom
Did the Caesars triumph? Byzantium lives in song,
Were all her dwellings palaces? And even in Atlantis of the
    legend
The night the sea rushed in,
The drowning men still bellowed for their slaves.

Young Alexander conquered India.
He alone?
Caesar beat the Gauls.
Was there not even a cook in his army?
Philip of Spain wept as his fleet
Was sunk and destroyed. Were there no other tears?
Frederick the Great triumphed in the Seven Years War. Who
Triumphed with him?

Each page a victory,
At whose expense the victory ball?
Every ten years a great man,
Who paid the piper?

So many particulars.
So many questions.

Bertolt Brecht

From SELECTED POEMS OF BERTOLT BRECHT translated by H.R. Hays. Copy-
right, 1947, by Bertolt Brecht and H.R. Hays. Reprinted by permission of Harcourt
Brace Jovanovich, Inc.

ACKNOWLEDGMENTS

This book addresses a central trend in advanced industrial societies: the shift of labor and capital from goods-producing industries to services. It examines, in particular, the patterns of this transformation during the twentieth century and discusses the sociological consequences of this process. A study of this nature obviously accrues many obligations, and much of my intellectual indebtedness will be evident in the book itself. But I would like to recognize here the special contributions of the following friends and colleagues.

The study was begun while I was at the University of Texas at Austin. Numerous discussions with members of the Population Research Center helped me in shaping the *problématique* of my study. I thank John Higley and Gideon Sjoberg for many valuable suggestions, and Joe Feagin for his continued support during the project. But most of all, I want to thank my friend Harley L. Browning for his many suggestions, criticisms, and encouragement; without them, this work would not have been possible. I am very fortunate that our paths continue to cross beyond the completion of this project: we are currently collaborating on a study of the transformation of the U.S. labor force.

I also want to thank Paul N. Rosenstein-Rodan for the great interest that he has shown in my work; his advice was invaluable for the economic segments of this analysis.

On leave from Vanderbilt University, I spent the year 1977 as a postdoctoral fellow at the Center for Demography and Ecology of the University of Wisconsin in Madison. My stay there gave me the necessary time to thoroughly revise the manuscript.

I would like to express my gratitude to Jim Sweet and Larry Bumpass for their generosity in making all facilities of the Center easily available to me. My many contacts with the members of the Center and the Department of Sociology, and their collegiality greatly contributed to the successful completion of the study. In particular, Manuel Castells and Erik Wright made many stimulating and challenging suggestions. Since the manuscript was almost completed at that time, only a few of their suggestions could be incorporated, but I hope that my current writings will do more justice to them.

Three other persons need to be mentioned from whose comments and critical readings of earlier drafts I greatly benefited: Peter Singelmann, Paul Singer, and Mayer N. Zald.

While the book was in press, I attended the International Symposium on the Service Sector of the Economy that was organized by Manuel Sigüenza in San Juan, Puerto Rico. The exchanges at that symposium were very stimulating, and the papers, particularly those dealing with socialist economies, provide an important extension to the concern of this study with advanced capitalist economies.

Various drafts of the book were typed by Joette Christianson and Janice Deneen. No matter how little time they had to complete the task, they somehow always managed to do it, and I would like to thank them for their unselfish assistance.

A short section of this book was earlier published as a paper in the *American Journal of Sociology* (Volume 83, March 1978), and I thank the University of Chicago Press for its permission to reprint those pages.

Finally, the completion of this study would have been much less enjoyable without the presence of Sylvia.

Chapter 1

INTRODUCTION

All countries, in the course of economic development, undergo changes in the composition of the labor force. Most prominently, these changes are reflected in both the occupational and the industry structures. Because the study of occupational changes aims directly at such aspects as status, prestige, and social stratification in general, it is not surprising that sociologists have been more concerned with occupations than industries. But there is a close interrelation between the occupational and industry structures of the labor force. In fact, a recent study of the United States labor force showed that during the 1960-1970 decade, two-thirds of all changes in the occupational structure resulted directly from differential growth of industries (Browning and Singelmann, 1975: Chapter 5). An analysis of changes in the industry structure of a country thus should add an important dimension to the study of social change.

The examination of long-term changes in the industry structure of industrialized countries leads to two broad generalizations. First, agricultural employment is steadily declining and second, all countries have experienced an increase of employment in service industries. In some countries, the proportion of agricultural employment has become so small that the rate of

decline is leveling off, but this is not yet the case with the rate
of increase of services. A recent comparison of employment
shifts in ten industrialized countries revealed that in 1970
service employment accounted for over 50 percent of total
employment in six of these countries (Sorrentino, 1971).

In contrast to the extensive documentation of the decline of
agricultural employment (e.g., Barkin, 1970; Rostow, 1969;
Kuznets, 1966; Schultz, 1964; Thomas, 1964; Clark, 1940),
much less is known about the growth of service industries.
Beside the classic studies by Fisher (1935) and Clark (1940),
the work by Bell (1973; 1976), Fuchs (1968; 1969), Graf
(1968), Greenfield (1966), and Menz (1965) are notable exceptions. In general, it is assumed that in the course of economic
development there is a sequential shift of employment from
agriculture and other extractive industries to manufacturing and
finally, to services. Contemporary evidence from developing
countries (Sabolo, 1975), however, shows no support for this
sequence, and an inspection of the data in Table 1.1 shows a
large variety of industry structures among countries at very
similar levels of economic growth. But with service industries
employing a growing share of the labor force—the U.S. figure
already is two-thirds—an examination of the development of
services becomes imperative.

Today the growth of services is at the cutting edge of many
economic and sociological issues. For example, productivity in
services is very difficult to measure (Fuchs, 1968; 1969), yet
the financial difficulties of many cities in the United States have
made the productivity and efficiency of municipal service
workers a major issue. As noted by the New York *Times* (March
2, 1977): "A new debate over a productivity plan for municipal
workers put forward by their unions and New York City has
once again raised basic questions of what productivity is and
how it can be measured in service industries such as
government."

The outcome of this debate, aside from its academic merits,
has immediate consequences for the workers, because cost-of-
living adjustments in their wages are tied to productivity increases.

Lately, the costs of many services (foremost among them are medical services) have risen much faster than prices for manufactured goods. With a growing share of personal expenditures spent on services, the issue of inflation becomes intimately tied to the wage-price spiral in the service industries. Complicating

Table 1.1: Sector Distribution of Employment: Twenty OECD Countries, 1960, and the United States, 1870-1960

Per Capita National Income (1960 U.S. dollars)	Country (in descending order of income)	Sector Distribution of Employment (percentages)		
		Agriculture	Industry	Service
2,132	United States 1960	8	38	54
1,836	United States 1950	12	39	48
1,536	Canada	13	43	45
1,644	Sweden	14	53	33
1,364	United States 1940	19	35	46
1,361	Switzerland	11	56	33
1,242	Luxembourg	15	51	34
1,170	United States 1930	22	36	42
1,105	United Kingdom	4	56	40
1,050	United States 1920	24	41	35
1,048	Denmark	18	45	37
1,035	West Germany	15	60	25
1,013	France	20	44	36
1,005	Belgium	6	52	42
977	Norway	20	49	32
927	United States 1910	28	38	34
839	Iceland	25	47	29
810	Netherlands	11	49	40
757	United States 1900	35	34	32
681	Austria	23	47	30
592	United States 1890	40	31	29
529	Ireland	36	30	34
504	Italy	27	46	28
499	United States 1880	47	27	26
344	Japan	33	35	32
340	United States 1870	47	27	26
324	Greece	56	24	20
290	Spain	42	37	21
238	Portugal	44	33	23
177	Turkey	79	12	9

Source: Fuchs, 1968: 30

the situation further is the fact that some segments of the service sector—notably the professions, such as lawyers, dentists, and physicians—have been able to a certain extent to shelter themselves from the market by controlling their own supply (less so in the case of lawyers) and by playing a significant role in the formation of policies affecting the demand for their services. This position undoubtedly has contributed to the spiraling costs of legal and medical services.

The growth of services has important implications for sociological analysis as well. The absence of a tangible product and the difficulty of stockpiling services, for example, require different organizations of work, as compared to goods-producing industries. Most services require little physical strength and this should remove a further barrier to the equal employment of women. It also should facilitate the employment of older workers, which is becoming even more important with the increase in the mandatory retirement age to seventy years.

One of the most important aspects of the growth of services is the expansion of the public sector and the welfare state (Janowitz, 1976; Wilensky, 1975). This segment of the service sector largely concerns health services, education, welfare, and public administration, which have been receiving vastly increased shares of total GNP through taxation and deficit spending. While the provision of these services has never been without controversy—not even in the heyday of the Great Society—the worldwide economic crisis of the 1970s has brought with it a renewed surge of criticism of these programs (see e.g., Rusher, 1974; Bacon and Eltis, 1976).

Often the growth of a service economy is seen as one signal for the "coming of postindustrial society" and the emergence of technological knowledge as a new basis for power in that society (Bell, 1973; 1976). Yet as Richta (1977: 52) noted: "This illusion behind these conceptions is that where power is armed with knowledge, it is eo ipso knowledge that controls power." Other areas in which the growth of services has the potential for important sociological changes is the role of the consumer in a service economy (Gartner and Riessman, 1974) and the conditions of work (Braverman, 1974; Mandel, 1972;

1968). With respect to many of these issues, there is a sharp division between the postindustrialists on the one hand, and the Marxists on the other. In general, postindustrialists view the emergence of a service economy as the harbinger of a more people-oriented society, whereas most Marxists would deny that a service economy would overcome the antagonisms of an industrial capitalist society. The arguments from both sides are relatively uninformed about the nature of the various service industries. Although it is not the purpose of this study to evaluate these two approaches, the information presented herein provides some of the data necessary for such evaluation.

In order to diminish the discrepancy between the emergence of services and our knowledge about their nature and differentiation, this book examines the sectoral transformation of the labor force in advanced capitalist countries during the period *circa* 1920-1970. The following four objectives are part of the analysis: (1) to describe the changes in the industry structure of employment that have taken place in the group of countries under investigation, with a special emphasis on the growth of service industries; (2) to analyze the relationship of the industry structure to per capita income, international trade, and urbanization; (3) to identify the path(s) of the sectoral transformation in the advanced industrial countries; and (4) to discuss some of the sociological consequences of this transformation of employment, such as changes in the occupational structure, the nature of work, the class structure, and international migration.

THE SELECTION OF THE COUNTRIES

The following seven countries were selected from the larger group of early industrialized countries: the United States, Canada, Great Britain, West Germany, France, Italy, and Japan. As a more detailed discussion of these countries is presented in Chapter 2, it will suffice for the present to state that all began their industrialization before the turn of the century.

The decision to restrict this study to advanced industrial countries was guided by several considerations. Sorrentino's (1971) study shows industrialized countries to have a very large proportion of their labor force in service industries. Moreover, these countries have a greater variety or mix of different services than do developing countries, i.e., their service employment has shifted from largely personal services—such as domestic service—to other types of service industries. Thus the central question is: "How did the current structure of service employment in the advanced industrial countries emerge?" This question can be answered by going back to the early part of this century. In that way, a study of industrialized countries can be made to detect the changes that take place in the service sector during the course of economic development.

Given such a knowledge of the emergence of the service sector and its changing structure in industrialized countries, it will be possible to show that countries might follow quite distinct patterns of the sectoral transformation of the labor force, depending on the time at which they started to industrialize, internal economic and demographic conditions, and their position within the system of international trade. For it is contended here (as will be elaborated later) that the early industrialized countries themselves do not follow one common pattern of labor force transformation. Such a finding has important consequences for our understanding of the late industrializing countries. In many developing countries today, the service sector is much larger than in the developed countries at comparable levels of development. This growth of services is often viewed in negative terms due to the implicit assumption that major growth of services should come after the expansion of the other economic sectors. But if the developed countries—usually thought of as a very homogenous group—themselves show clear differences in the way their services expanded, there would be less reason to use the experience of the developed countries as a yardstick for contemporary development. Thus, the question is: "Does one of the historical patterns serve as a guideline for the late industrializing countries, or will they have to follow their own pattern(s)?" Since the current conditions for the late developing countries are very different from those that existed in Europe or North America in the last century, differences between the two groups of countries are to be expected. This leaves us with the seemingly paradoxical situation where we need to know more about the patterns of the labor force transformation in the early industrialized countries in order to understand why these patterns cannot be repeated. This study strives to provide not only a documentation of the changing industry allocation of employment in the course of economic development but also to serve as a starting point for a more general analysis of employment changes that would include countries whose industrialization began during different time periods.

Two other comments about the selection of the seven countries need to be made. First, although other mature industrial countries such as Belgium or Switzerland might have been chosen as well, the problem of finding the necessary data mandated a limitation of the number of countries that could be included in the study. However, the final seven countries that were selected truly represent the group of advanced capitalist countries, for they *are* the *major* countries with capitalist economies. These countries consult among each other regularly about international economic issues, as illustrated by the meetings of their heads of government in London in 1977 and Bonn in 1978. Furthermore, countries such as the United States, West Germany, and Japan are commonly viewed as locomotives to stimulate economic growth in the Western world. Even Italy with its shaky political and economic situation is vital to the international capitalist system, which is one of the reasons why the other countries are so concerned about who participates in the Italian government.

Second, it was also decided to exclude noncapitalist countries from the analysis. Again, as in the case of developing countries, a comparison between capitalist and socialist/communist countries would have been very interesting. But such comparison would add so many additional aspects to the analysis, starting with the industry allocation of employment, that it would go beyond the scope that is possible here. Once more information about different groups of countries is amassed, it will be possible to contrast the sectoral transformation of the labor force in different social systems.

The Time Period and Data

Given the specific concern of the analysis with the emergence and growth of service industries, the period from 1920 to 1970 has been selected as the time framework. Ideally, the investigation should go as far back as the middle of the nineteenth century in order to capture the expansion of domestic service as one of the largest single industries, if not the largest, but the quality of census data (particularly on the comparative level) does not permit extending the period further back. As will be seen in Chapter 3, the quality of the data for the 1920s and 1930s leaves much to be desired. But these five decades nevertheless include the time when services began to grow at an above average rate, and they also include the historical point when services for the first time accounted for over one-half of total employment in a country (the United States), thus signaling what some writers have called a service economy (Fuchs, 1968) or a postindustrial society (Bell, 1973).

In order to examine the changing industry structure in terms of detailed industries, an extensive acquisition and processing of labor force trends in the seven countries is necessary, owing to the scarcity of information available on this subject. For this purpose, no detailed information could be obtained from international data sources such as the United Nations *Statistical Yearbooks,* and even the annual statistical publications of the seven countries proved inadequate with respect to their detail of information about industry categories. There are, of course, a number of studies that deal with the decline of agricultural employment (Schultz, 1964), the nature and problems of industrial societies (Faunce, 1968; Kindleberger, 1969; Bain, 1966), or the emergence of a service-oriented economy (Fuchs, 1968), but most of these studies are restricted to general trends and to the use of broad industry categories such as agriculture, manufacturing, and services. In those cases were more detailed information is provided, the differentiation is usually restricted to manufacturing. A good example of this situation is the *Yearbook of Labor Statistics* published by the International Labor Office which contains a great deal of information about detailed manufacturing industries but, surprisingly, has little information about services. In the words of Greenfield (1966: 1), "The size and significance of the service sector nothwithstanding, it has only recently been studied in depth." Fuchs' book, *The Service Economy* (1968), still is the best empirical study of services in the United States, although he, too, used only gross categories.

Therefore, it was decided to use the labor force data from all national censuses that were taken by the seven countries since 1920. This task involved the processing of 38 individual censuses (the European countries did not conduct a census during World War II). In each case, the most detailed industry classification was used (which either was a three-digit or a four-digit industry classification), and these employment data were then aggregated to make each census comparable over time and cross-nationally. (This procedure is discussed in detail in this chapter in the section on the industry allocation scheme.) This processing of the data permits the discrimination of different types of service industries necessary for a meaningful evaluation of international differences in industry structure. Two countries, for example, may have the same proportion of their labor force employed in services but one country might have a concentration in personal services, while the second country features strong business and social services sectors. Although of identical size in terms of employment, the function of the service sector for the total economy will vastly differ in the two countries. Without such detailed information about service industries, the relationship between industries cannot be specified.

Linkages Among Industries:
Capital, Output, and Employment

Some work in terms of detailed information about different service industries has already been done (Hultgren, 1948; Barger, 1951; Fabricant, 1952; Goldsmith, 1958; Greenfield, 1966). In particular, the great importance of social overhead industries, such as transportation and communication, for the sustained development of the manufacturing sector has been well documented (Rosenstein-Rodan, 1943; Hirschman, 1958; Nurkse, 1970). While these social overhead industries require

large amount of capital (and feature some of the highest capital-output ratios), their growth nonetheless is reflected in the
number of people they employ.

The relationship of social overhead industries to other sectors
and industries of the economy represents a "linkage," to use
Hirschman's (1958) terminology. The function of linkages
maintains a prominent place in economic theories of development, primarily within the context of capital requirements. This
is particularly important in those cases where capital is scarce
and a decision must be made as to where to invest the available
capital in an efficient and growth-stimulating way. Once certain
industries are identified as possessing a high propensity for
growth incentives to other industries, capital investments in
these industries will receive priority on the part of the state: "[I] t
is the experience of unbalanced growth in the past that pro-
duces, at an advanced stage of economic development, the
possibility of balanced growth" (Hirschman, 1958: 93).

Hirschman distinguishes between two kinds of linkages. *Back-
ward* linkages can be thought of as a reliance of one industry on
goods from another industry (or set of industries). A boom in
railroad construction, for example, would require an increased
output of rails and other metal products. *Forward* linkages refer
to the fact that "every activity that does not by its nature cater
exclusively to final demands, will induce attempts to utilize its
outputs as inputs in some new activities" (Hirschman, 1958:
100). Forward linkages of railroads, therefore, are those services
which are bought by other industries in order to distribute
goods to the final consumer. The concept of linkages by no
means is restricted to social overhead capital; Fishlow
(1965:288), for example, examined the forward linkages of
agriculture to agricultural processing industries.

There are many linkages between a certain group of services
(including trade, financing, insurance, and business services) and
industries in other sectors, for a large segment of these activities
caters not to individual consumers but to other firms. Thus,
close attention will be given to the relative growth rate of the
various industries and their relationship over time.

But the form of linkages pursued in this study differs somewhat from the economic approach as developed by Hirschman

(1958). The preceding examples demonstrated that capital and output are vital concepts for economic analyses of interindustry relationships. Through an input-output matrix, changes in output can be linked to changes in employment. Conventionally this is done by estimating the effects of a certain increment of sales in a given industry on the generation of employment in that industry and, in all other industries (including an estimation of the multiplier effect). But obviously, the nature of these effects is neither constant over time nor necessarily identical among countries. Given the scope of this study, it would have been impossible to construct comparable input-output matrices for all countries during each census year since 1920. Thus, this analysis is restricted to the examination of employment and its transformation.

This perspective obviously will assign different weights to industries than would an analysis concentrating on output. Consider the case of utility industries, for example, which are essential for the growth of manufacturing activities and therefore have many forward linkages. Owing to their high capital-output ratio, their importance for the entire economy is not readily visible in terms of employment. Similarly, the fact that employment in transportation has remained relatively constant or has even declined in recent times does not imply that the linkage function has diminished; the function is only increasingly performed by capital instead of labor.

But the nature of the relationship between industries, as defined in this study, differs in yet another way from the economic approach to linkages. The concern here is not with changes in absolute employment but with the relative shares of total employment allocated to industries, and their changes over time. This means, of course, that by definition a change in one industry is accompanied by a change in another industry (or set of industries), and this does not necessarily imply a cause-and-effect relationship. The importance of relative employment shares and their change in the course of economic development lies in the fact that the labor force gets proportionately redistributed among industries and, concomitantly, different occupations. These changes affect the structural conditions for social mobility, the organization of work, and many other spheres that are of sociological importance. Moreover, the requirements of capital accumulation impose increasing problems for the continuous creation of new employment opportunities; in order to avoid even higher rates of unemployment than already exist today (which even in West Germany, with its traditional full-employment situation, is over 4 percent), the state may be forced to increasingly provide services and employment opportunities. This situation already is emerging in parts of the United States. Since the 1960s, for example, a large number of corporations have moved from the Northeastern region to the South and, as a result, the Northeast has had the highest rate of expansion of social services of all regions.

As Fuchs (1968:183) reminded us: "labor is human and physical capital is not; it is appropriate, therefore, to give labor primary attention in any broad study concerned with total social development." The analysis of relationships between employment changes among industries must, therefore, be viewed as complementary to the economic concern with linkages. Despite the fact that an industry can maintain its linkage function over a given time period, the nature of the association, between employment in that industry and employment in those industries with which it maintains linkages, can change during that same time.

Economic Development, Labor Force Changes,
and the Industry Allocation Scheme

It is clear by now that a successful investigation of the industry structure of employment requires information about detailed industries, in order to assess the relative size and its change of all branches of the economy, particularly with respect to service industries. At the same time, however, the various industries must be allocated to a limited number of sectors if possible patterns of these changes, i.e., the sectoral transformation, are to be detected. A brief review of existing industry allocation schemes will make it apparent why they are of limited utility for this study, and the remainder of this chapter thus discusses an alternative scheme that forms the conceptual basis for the analyses in Chapters 3 to 5.

In the past, various attempts have been made to classify industries into a manageable number of broad industry groups in order to detect changes in the distribution of the labor force over time. Most of these divisions form a three-sector model (e.g. Wolfe, 1955; Fourastié, 1966), and the idea of a tripartite division of industries in effect can be traced back to the Swiss census of 1888 (Menz, 1965). But it was the scheme advanced by A.G.B. Fisher (1935) and Colin Clark (1940) which became most widely used in the literature (see Fuchs, 1968), perhaps due in part to the simplicity of their sectoral allocation and the way they suggested that it becomes transformed. The Fisher-Clark model consists of the following three sectors:

(1) *Primary* industries (agriculture, fishing, forestry, mining)

(2) *Secondary* industries (manufacturing, construction, utilities)

(3) *Tertiary* industries (commerce, transport, communication, services)

Any classification, of course, must be evaluated in its substantive context. Depending on the specific problem, one or another classification is useful, and no sector allocation scheme can claim to be equally effective in all situations. It was the intent of both Fisher and Clark to analyze the relationship between economic development and changes in the industry structure of the labor force, and their classification therefore must be examined in those terms.

A.G.B. Fisher (1935:7) stated the following relationship:

We may say that in every progressive economy there has been a steady shift of employment and investment from the essential "primary" activities, without whose products life in even its most primitive forms would be impossible, to secondary activities of all kinds, and to a still greater extent into tertiary production. . . .

The shifts of employment toward secondary and tertiary production revealed by the census are the inescapable reflection of economic progress.

And in a similar vein, Colin Clark (1940:6-7) wrote:

> Studying economic progress in relation to the economic structure of
> different countries, we find a firmly established generalization that a
> high average level of real income per head is always associated with a
> high proportion of the working population engaged in tertiary
> industries.

Colin Clark's and A.G.B. Fisher's approach is evaluated by
Postan (1971:86) in the following manner: "In Clark's formulation the tripartite order of sectors was transformed from a
mere classification into an itinerary of economic progress. The
lesson he taught was that economic progress had been achieved
in the past and was to be achieved in the future by transferring
resources first from primary occupations to secondary ones and,
finally, from secondary to tertiary ones." These resources include physical capital as well as human capital. And he continues: "Colin Clark, in his *Conditions of Economic Progress,*
has done more than anyone else to give currency to the notion
that the income in the primary occupations (mainly agriculture
and extracting industries) is always lower than in the secondary
and tertiary occupations. From this classification it naturally
follows that in order to attain the main purpose of economic
development, which is higher income per head, it is necessary in
periods of planned growth to channel into industry the bulk of
disposible resources" (Postan, 1971:105). Postan noted that
Clark himself acknowledged in several places that the marginal
productivity in agricultural and extractive industries is not
always lower than the product in other industries. In some
countries such as Belgium or Great Britain, the transfer of
employment from agriculture to industry may not change the
national product very much, whereas in other countries like
Denmark or New Zealand such a transfer might even lower
national product. In short, both Fisher and Clark used the
three-sector classification of industries in order to demonstrate
that economic growth of nations is closely associated with the
transfer of employment from industries with low productivity
to those with high productivity.

Fisher and Clark were the first to call attention to the fact that the industry structure of the labor force changes in the course of economic development. But, as pioneers in the field, they could not do much more than roughly sketch the pattern by which the labor force becomes transformed.

The Fisher-Clark thesis has been criticized on several grounds, many of which are more a matter of emphasis than of substance. (A good example is the discussion between Fisher (1952; 1954), on the one side, and Bauer and Yamey [1951; 1954] and Triantes [1953], on the other.) For instance, a charge has been leveled against Fisher and Clark that their three-sector model fails to identify the service functions of primary and secondary industries. However, this criticism can be directed against all industry classification schemes based on conventional data, for as long as the census bureaus do not report the proportion of "hidden" service employment in non-service industries, this shortcoming can hardly be avoided. But even granted this inadequacy of classification, a substantial increase in the proportion of service employment over time still shows up, in spite of the understatement of some service activities.

Two important criticisms of the Fisher-Clark thesis, however, merit special attention. First, historical and contemporary evidence demonstrates that a decline of agricultural employment is not always accompanied by a growth of primarily secondary industries. It can result in a direct increase in tertiary employment (Oshima, 1971). Even Clark's own data show that many countries do not follow the postulated pattern. In addition, although there is a direct relationship for each country between the level of per capita income and the proportion of tertiary employment, this relationship is much weaker crossnationally (cf., Table 1.1).

The most important shortcoming of the Fisher-Clark thesis has been pointed out by Bauer and Yamey (1951), who noted that the relationship between per capita income and the proportion of tertiary employment lacks a theoretical basis because of the heterogeneity of industries within the tertiary sector. Consider only the differences between economic activities such as transportation, banking and financing, and domestic service, all of which belong to the teritary sector. What do these services have in common (other than the fact that they do not produce a tangible product) to suggest that their role in economic development, and the labor force trends resulting from it, are comparable enough to permit an undifferentiated analysis of services? Truly, these industries differ along many dimensions, be it in their capital input, size of establishment, or nature of output, to name only a few. Thus, while some service industries can be positively associated with rising per capita income, others show a negative association. This is a very important point that is frequently overlooked whenever changes in the labor force are examined in a three-sector scheme.

This basic ambiguity of the tertiary sector indicates the need for a new industry allocation scheme, which would permit a higher degree of differentiation than is the case with the traditional three-sector model. In the literature very few attempts have been made to arrive at a new allocation scheme, probably owing to the scant attention which the sectoral transformation of the labor force has received over the past twenty years. Besides the original Fisher-Clark formulation and the subsequent series of criticisms and rebuttals referred to above, only a few conceptual articles on the subject have appeared (e.g., Sengupta, 1958).

Despite the widespread critique of the Fisher-Clark model and the consensus among economists about its limited utility, most empirical studies of the labor force continue to use the traditional three-sector scheme (Kuznets, 1957; Bairoch and Limbur, 1968; Sabolo, 1969) with only minor variations, such as the exclusion of transportation and communication from other services. When more detailed information is given (Kuznets, 1971), this is usually restricted to the broad (one-digit) industry groups of the International Standard Industry Classification (ISIC) established by the United Nations (1958) as a guide for national census bureaus. This classification includes the following nine industry groups

(1) Agriculture, forestry, hunting, and fishing

(2) Mining and quarrying

(3) Manufacturing

(4) Construction

(5) Electricity, gas, water, and sanitary services

(6) Commerce

(7) Transport, storage, and communication

(8) Services

(9) Industries not elsewhere classified (n.e.c.)

While the intent of this classification to provide a sufficient degree of international comparability (at least on the level of broad industry groups) is certainly commendable, the major shortcoming of the traditional three-sector model is still present, namely its heterogeneity within the sectors. Although commerce, transportation and communication are listed separately, the industry group of "services" continues to contain a great number of very different economic activities. As far as a study of services is concerned, the ISCI does not represent a great improvement over the Fisher-Clark model.

Since 1971, however, a renewed interest in this topic has emerged and more attention has been given to empirical documentation of sectoral employment changes, especially the shift towards services. Probably the two most interesting recent attempts to distinguish between different kinds of services and to allocate them to economic sectors have been generated by Katouzian (1971) and Singer (1971).

Following Bauer and Yamey's (1951) notion of the heterogeneous character of the tertiary sector, whereby some service industries may grow in the course of economic development while others decline, Katouzian suggests a division of the tertiary sector into three categories: (1) complementary services, (2) new services, and (3) old services.

Complementary services. This category includes banking, finance, transportation, wholesale and retail trade. This sector is most closely linked to the transformative industries, and its services "expand in response to a rise in demand in a new productive situation" (Katouzian, 1971:366). It is expected that these services sharply increase after the Industrial Revolution but their growth will diminish as the economy develops to the point where a slight decline may occur in a post-industrial society.

> These services have been complementary to the growth of manufacturing production in two ways: as complementary factors to urbanization, and as necessary links to the process of round-about or capitalistic production. The growing demand for labour in industrial centres attracted migrants to urban areas, and factory production necessitated a high degree of urbanization. The growth of round-about production increased the range and complexity of intermediate goods and (with the underlying specialization process that was taking place) it helped the conversion of local markets into a unified national market and expanded foreign trade—all demanding services included in this category. Therefore, as the rate of growth of industrial production increased, so did the rate of growth of these services, and vice versa (Katouzian, 1971:366-367).

New services. This cateogry "includes education, consumption of modern clinical and medical services, entertainments in general (including holiday resorts, hotels, restaurants, cinemas, concerts, nightclubs, and the like), and such other services that may be appropriately included in this category" (Katouzian, 1971:366). These services are labeled new because of the recent feature of mass consumption in advanced industrialized countries, whereas in earlier phases of industrialization the demand for those services was mainly restricted to the aristocracy.

> The demand for these services is highly sensitive to the growth of *per capita* incomes, and it is also an increasing function of the amount of *per capita* leisure-time (especially if the community curve of the distribution of leisure-time is not lopsided) (Katouzian, 1971: 366).

Old services. "The group of services in this category consists of those activities which flourished before industrialization and whose importance and contribution has almost continuously declined since" (Katouzian, 1971: 367). One of the largest industries in this category is domestic service, and its share of the labor force has steadily declined. Although Katouzian is not very explicit about the services to be included in this category, he seems to refer mainly to personal service.

Applying his scheme to labor force changes in a number of industrialized countries, Katouzian demonstrates that part of the Fisher-Clark thesis is valid: "We have agreed that the demand for the New Services begins to rise with the growth of per capita incomes, above some critical level, and will normally continue to grow with the increase in incomes, the expansion of leisure-time, as well as a redistribution of these in favor of the majority of the population" (Katouzian, 1971:368). The old services, in contrast, begin to decline when new services increase, and both new services and complementary services take over part of the functions of the old services. Complementary services, according to Katouzian, grow in direct response to manufacturing development, but the growth rate of individual complementary services can vary. Transportation, for instance, is more likely to expand during the initial stages of industrialization, while banking and finance services rise, in terms of employment at least, when manufacturing industries have reached a certain volume.

The different trends of various kinds of services make it clear that a study of the labor force in general, and of services in particular, must indeed divide the traditional tertiary sector into more homogeneous service sectors in order to evaluate the shift of the labor force towards services. As Katouzian put it (1971:369):

> The aggregate behaviour of these categories will determine the overall share of the service sector at any stage. Categories II and III change basically as a result of industrialization and development and hence their behaviour bears no *direct* relation to changes in *per capita* incomes. Therefore it may be safe to suggest that the relative concentration observed in the long-term trend of the Old Services has been falling, the share of the Complementary Services has been

increasing *at a declining rate,* and only the share of the New Services has been continuously rising with increases in *per capita* incomes.

In contrast to Katouzian's analysis of industrialized countries, Paulo Singer (1971) studied changes in the Brazilian labor force from 1920 to 1968 and he, too, derived a new sectoral allocation scheme, again emphasizing the need for a differentiation of the traditional tertiary sector. Since the context of his study differs from the present analysis, it may suffice to show here that his sector divisions are very comparable to that of Katouzian. Singer divides the traditional tertiary industries into the following sectors: (1) production services (commerce transportation, communication, warehousing); (2) collective consumption services (government, education, health, and other social services); and (3) individual consumption services (liberal professions, domestic services, repair services, and other personal services). Singer's main objective was to detect differences within the tertiary sector during the course of Brazilian economic development. As in the case of Katouzian, these labor force shifts are seen as reflections of the changing economy, as a whole, rather than as necessary stages for development.

These two illustrations suggest that a study of the labor force in relation to economic development cannot be executed with the traditional three-sector model. While it would have been possible to utilize either the Katouzian or the Singer scheme in this study, it was decided to employ a third industry allocation scheme. At the beginning of this study, neither of the two schemes discussed above were known to this author, and it was only during the investigation that he came across these earlier classifications. For apparent reasons this study could not have been carried out with the traditional tripartite scheme, so a new industry allocation model had to be developed in the early stages of this investigation. (It should be acknowledged here that the original formulation of that new allocation scheme was presented by Harley L. Browning in a seminar on the demogaphy of the labor force, in which the present author participated. We coauthored a number of papers in the following years during which this allocation scheme underwent some changes. This scheme, besides being utilized in this study, is currently used in a more detailed analysis of the labor force in the United States.)

The fact that a useful classification was already at hand is hardly sufficient reason in itself for preferring it in favor of either Katouzian's or Singer's scheme. But even a tripartite division of the traditional service sector will not suffice for international comparative purposes. In particular, the complementary services sector in Katouzian's scheme and the production services sector in Singer's scheme contain a number of quite different services, and Katouzian himself acknowledged their differential development (1971:368-369). And since transportation, communication, and trade, at least in industrialized countries, account for about 15-22 percent of the total labor force, a differentiation of this sector also makes sense empirically. It is therefore believed that the industry allocation scheme which is made up of six major industry sectors is the most useful one for the present study. This industry allocation scheme is given in Table 1.2, and the remainder of this chapter will be devoted to a discussion of the rationale for dividing industries in the manner proposed.

As Table 1.2 demonstrates, thirty-seven intermediate industry groups are classified into six sectors. For a broad cross-national analysis of the labor force, there are too many detailed industries to permit a meaningful comparison. Moreover, the number of detailed industries reported by national census bureaus has increased over time in all countries. At the other extreme, the reported broad industry groups (at the one-digit level) do not sufficiently discriminate service activities, as was discussed earlier. Even the intermediate industry groups (at the two-digit level, e.g., food industries as a further division of manufacturing, or insurance as a subdivision of commerce) are not very useful in the form reported by national censuses, for their content can vary from country to country. Retail trade in Japan and the United States, for example, includes eating and drinking places, whereas other countries allocate these services to hotels and lodging places. Therefore, it was decided to combine the available information on the most detailed industries into thirty-seven intermediate industry groups. This procedure guaranteed a maximal comparability, since the content of the intermediate categories could be determined independently. At the same time, these intermediate industries are still detailed enough to permit a thorough analysis of differences in the industry structure of the seven selected countries. However, more important than the problem of making detailed industries comparable is the question of how to allocate them into internally homogeneous industry sectors.

The first two sectors of the allocation scheme in Table 1.2 follow the traditional approach.* The primary industries in the Fisher-Clark model form the *Extractive* sector, while the secondary industries constitute the *Transformative* sector. It would have been possible, of course, to distinguish between more than the present six manufacturing industries, but information for this sector can be obtained from other studies (e.g.,Bain,1968), and given the particular interest of this study in the emergence of services, only the more important manufacturing industries are identified.

Following the sequential flow from extraction to transformation, the third industry sector is *Distributive services,* which includes transportation, communication, wholesale and retail trade. The sequence extraction-transformation-distribution, then, reflects the development of goods from the most undifferentiated primary form to their distribution to the ultimate customer. At each stage within this sequence, the use value of the product is increased. The remaining sectors lack this sequential flow, but they do form three distinct groups of industries.

The fourth sector, *Producer services,* is made up mainly, if not exclusively, of those industries that provide services to producers of goods or that are concerned with various forms of property. In that sense, they "are in the nature of intermediate

---

*Parts of this section are taken from another article entitled "The Emergence of a Service Society in the United States" (Browning and Singelmann, 1978).

Table 1.2: Allocation Scheme for Sectors and Industries

I. Extractive
- (1) Agriculture, fishing and forestry
- (2) Mining

II. Transformative
- (3) Construction
- (4) Food
- (5) Textile
- (6) Metal
- (7) Machinery
- (8) Chemical
- (9) Miscellaneous manufacturing
- (10) Utilities

III Distributive Services
- (11) Transportation and storage
- (12) Communication
- (13) Wholesale trade
- (14) Retail trade (except eating and drinking places)

IV. Producer Services
- (15) Banking, credit, and other financial services
- (16) Insurance
- (17) Real estate
- (18) Engineering and architectural services
- (19) Accounting and bookkeeping
- (20) Miscellaneous business services
- (21) Legal services

V. Social Services
- (22) Medical and health services
- (23) Hospitals
- (24) Education
- (25) Welfare and religious services
- (26) Nonprofit organizations
- (27) Postal services
- (28) Government
- (29) Miscellaneous professional and social services

VI. Personal Services
- (30) Domestic services
- (31) Hotels and lodging places
- (32) Eating and drinking places
- (33) Repair services
- (34) Laundry and dry cleaning
- (35) Barber and beauty shops
- (36) Entertainment and recreational services
- (37) Miscellaneous personal services

Source: Browning and Singelmann, 1975: Table I-1.

and not final output" (Greenfield, 1966:11). The nature of these services is very clearly shown by Machlup (1962:39-40):

> The services of certified public accountants, marketing research organizations and consulting engineers are sold almost entirely to business firms. Whether the firms buying these services use them for producing consumer goods or capital goods [durable producer goods] does not matter for our purposes; in either case, the production of knowledge serves in the current production of other things and the cost of the production of knowledge will be part of the cost of these other things, not a separate item in the national product, gross or net. The services of consulting engineers will perhaps be used more often in connection with new construction than with the current production of manufactured goods, and it might be interesting to see what portions of the investment in new plants are payments for knowledge produced in its planning and design. The services of architects are altogether of this sort; whether for industrial or residential construction, they furnish knowledge to be embodied in durable assets and the cost of this knowledge becomes part of the investment in fixed plant or dwellings.

The emergence of these industries is a result of increasing specialization of establishments and their complex organization. As was pointed out by Fuchs (1968), activities such as accounting or advertising once were performed within the organizations at earlier stages of industrial development, and their emergence as separate industries is tied in with the development of economies of scale.

Both distributive and producer services can be thought of as goods-oriented services in that they cater largely to commodities or to matters related with commodities and property. In contrast to these kind of services, the remaining service industries are primarily consumption-oriented. As such, all these services cater to the individual in one form or another, but it is precisely the different form through which these services are rendered that necessitates their differentiation, analogous to the division of the goods-oriented services into two sectors.

The fifth sector is made up of *Social services* which include health and medical services, education, and government, among others. These services are the new services, to use Katouzian's terminology, in the sense that their mass consumption is a relatively recent phenomena. While they do cater to the individual, their emergence is only partly the result of individual demand. More important for their growth is the collective demand, at least in industrialized countries, in terms of the idea of social welfare, health standards, and other social legislation. It follows, therefore, that social services are less oriented toward individualistic demands but rather toward individuals as a collective entity, be it the neighborhood, the community, the state, or even the nation. While this may fit education or government better than private medical services, they, too, are influenced by legislation enabling a large part of the population to make use of them than would otherwise have had the means to do so. This does not mean, of course, that there are no longer any differences among persons in their ability to utilize social services. But as the case of access to medical services suggests, these differences have diminished. Moreover, many persons who are not eligible for governmental health plans are covered by private plans, and since these are often part and parcel of employment contracts, their purchase, too, differs from other expenditures.

In terms of the function of social services, however, a distinction between two different types must be made: (1) activities serving the reproduction of labor power (basically health, hospitals, education, and welfare) and, (2) activities that primarily function to maintain the existing social relations among classes (police, public administration). In some ways, education serves both functions: besides providing people with necessary skills, it also is a socializing agent and keeps surplus labor from entering the labor force.

This discussion of the nature of social services demonstrates that an interpretation of the growth of this sector must take the nature of the state into account. Changes in social service employment reflect actions by the state which, in turn, result from the specific outcome of competing interests within social classes. Thus, the social service sector is an important manifestation of the role of the state in society.

The last sector, *Personal services,* is a residual category including many different heterogeneous economic activities,
which range from shoeshining to entertainment and recreational
services. But as was mentioned above, all these services are
characterized by their orientation towards the individual consumer. In contrast to social services, these services strongly
respond to supply and demand forces, a fact that was already
observed by Katouzian (1971). This sector, moreover, differs
from social services in many other respects such as forms of
organization, occupational distribution, and educational attainment of persons in this sector. In general, the size of personal
services is relatively small, a high proportion of blue collar
workers can be observed, and persons employed in personal
services are characterized by a relatively low educational
attainment.

Although neither the Katouzian or the Singer industry allocation scheme is used in this study, a comparison of them with
the Browning-Singelmann categories demonstrates that the possibilities to differentiate between different kinds of services are
apparently limited. Though the labels are different, the three
classifications are strikingly similar, and they can be grouped as
follows:

Browning and Singelmann	Katouzian	Singer
(1) Distributive services		
	(1) Complementary services	(1) Production services
(2) Producer services		
(3) Social services	(2) New services	(2) Collective consumption services
(4) Personal services	(3) Old services	(3) Individual consumption services

Finally, it is acknowledged that the allocation of three industries presented some difficulties: construction, retail trade,
and domestic service. Construction differs from other transformative industries in several ways. It is much less capital-
intensive than manufacturing, not to mention utilities, its average size of establishment is much smaller, and the work sched-

ule of construction varies much more than in other industries. During the outdoor season, a workday of 14 hours is no exception, while sometimes no work at all is possible during periods of hard freeze. The large size of construction employment, which accounts for about 5-8 percent of the labor force in industrialized countries, would permit a separation of construction from transformative industries and its classification as a separate sector.

However, several reasons question the separation of construction from the transformative sector. Because construction fits other sectors even less, the only alternative would be to treat it as an independent sector. Although the size of this industry would permit such a procedure empirically, that alternative has been rejected on conceptual grounds, for all other industry sectors consist of a number of industries. Moreover, the rationale behind the use of sectors instead of a larger number of broad industry groups is that sectors permit a better analysis of the transformation of the labor force over time, and it would be difficult to interpret this transformation without aggregate categories. After all, the popularity of the Fisher-Clark scheme was not unrelated to the simplicity of the sectors. Thus, there is a certain value in limiting the number of sectors to a manageable size.

The difficulty of allocating retail trade to the distributive services sector results from the fact that this service is a final output, for retail trade caters to the individual consumer. But in the context of the present study, data problems prevent a different allocation of retail trade, because most countries do not report separate employment figures for wholesale and retail trade prior to World War II. In the case of Great Britain, a distinction between these two types of trade is not even possible for 1960. No estimate of the proportion of retail trade can be made either, since the ratio of wholesale trade to retail trade varies over time and from country to country. Again, while the allocation of retail trade to distributive services sector is not fully satisfying, it is believed to be the best alternative available.

It will be remembered from the previous discussion that some countries include eating and drinking places in retail trade.

While the sale of food and beverages in a cafeteria, for example, can be classified as retail activity, in the sense of distributing a good to the final customer, the nature of these activities is quite distinct from other retailing. Employment in this industry is more comparable to other personal services in that it replaces a certain form of household work. In the course of economic development, more and more work traditionally carried out within the household itself is either greatly reduced by modern electrical appliances, or it is taken out of the household and performed by one personal service or another. In many respects eating and drinking places have much in common with hotels and lodging places, which are classified as a personal service in all censuses. For these reasons and due to the fact that some countries indeed do not distinguish between eating and drinking places, and hotels and lodging places (which often feature restaurant service themselves), it was decided to exclude the former industry from retail trade and to allocate it to the personal services sector.

These allocation difficulties demonstrate the importance of considering, besides employment changes across sectors, changes in the composition of industries within sectors, because not all industries in the same sector exhibit the same rate of growth. It is well known, for example, that in modern economies some manufacturing industries decline (such as textiles or food) while others increase (chemicals or machinery, for example). Similarly, the historical decline of domestic service from one of the largest individual industries to one of neglegible size must be taken into account, if one is to comprehend the employment trend of the personal services sector. For that reason, the subsequent labor force analysis will include a discussion, where necessary, of the thirty-seven separate industry groups.

With this exposition of the processing of the labor force data and their industry allocation, we can now turn to a more detailed discussion of the seven countries and their sectoral transformations of employment.

Chapter 2

THE CONDITIONS OF INDUSTRIALIZATION

IN THE SEVEN COUNTRIES

The transformation of the labor force from agriculture to services is one of the main facets of economic development. By 1920, industrialization was well under way in all seven countries of this study, but its level varied widely among the countries. For example, Italy and Japan still had more than one-half of their labor forces in extractive industries, compared with only one-seventh in England. The different levels of industrialization in 1920, of course, reflect the differences among the countries in the pattern of economic development prior to the 1920-1970 period. Thus, to provide a better understanding of the economic situation the seven countries were facing at the beginning of that period, it is the purpose of this chapter to discuss some developmental aspects prior to 1920. In addition, some country-specific developments that can shed light on the changes in the industry structure will be addressed for the 1920-1970 period. Obviously, economic development is too broad a topic to be fully discussed for the seven countries in this one chapter. Such comparison would constitute a study in its own. Rather, the objective here is to provide some of the economic and political features (such as the development of the key industries in a particular economy or the formation of a nation state) that are related to the sectoral transformation of the labor force. (The sources referred to in this chapter provide a formidable introduction for those who would like to familiarize themselves more with the topic of industrialization in the seven countries.)

Changes in Production and Employment, 1850-1920

UNITED STATES

It has been noted that for many decades following the end of colonial rule, the economy of the United States remained predominantly oriented toward agriculture. "The nation got its first start as an agricultural economy producing a surplus for exports and depending upon imports for most of its manufactured goods" (Peterson and Gray, 1969:286). During these years the volume of exports never reached the volume of imports, and a positive balance of payments was made possible only through shipping services performed for other nations and by attracting foreign capital (Peterson and Gray, 1969:297). Despite considerable economic progress in the early nineteenth century, the gross national product of the United States remained well below that of either Britain or France until the mid-century (Davis et al., 1972:33). But the comparatively low GNP does not reflect the rising productivity of the agricultural industries, which provided a sound basis for the subsequent rise of other industry sectors. By the middle of the nineteenth century manufacturing industries expanded significantly, thereby indicating the forthcoming shift from a predominantly agricultural economy to an industrial economy. This industrial growth came to a momentary halt with the outbreak of the Civil War, but shortly after its end the economy recovered very quickly and grew at the highest rate the country had ever seen (Davis et al., 1972:447).

Although industrialization had started late in the first half of the nineteenth century, the Civil War is commonly regarded as the dividing mark between the United States as an agricultural economy and as an industrial economy (Bagwell and Mingay, 1970:11). During the three decades from 1830 to 1860, for example, 30,000 miles of railroads were built, clearly demonstrating the onset of industrialization in the United States. Compared with the subsequent rate of expansion, however, this was only the beginning. In the thirty years from 1860 to 1890 an additional 140,000 miles were completed (Davis et al., 1972:500). Associated with the rapid growth of the economy in the postwar period were the rising number of land grants to railroad companies, the emergence of a national banking system, and high tariffs protecting the new American manufacturing industries. Bagwell and Mingay (1970:165) point out, however, that the growth of the American economy was primarily due to improved technology. Once it was applied to the vast natural resources of this nation, tariffs lost much of their importance and played only a subordinate role for further growth.

While the expansion of railroads in the period following the Civil War probably is the most dramatic indicator of the rate of economic growth during that time, other developments are remarkable as well. "The value added in manufacturing production began to exceed the value of agricultural commodities in the mid-1880's" (Peterson and Gray, 1969:286), and by the end of the nineteenth century manufacturing accounted for over half of the total commodity output (Davis et al., 1972:252). The increasing importance of manufacturing also is reflected in the trade statistics; while it contributed only about 15 percent to all exports until 1880, its share rose to 50 percent by 1920 (Peterson and Gray, 1969:298). In general, the shift of the labor force in this period, from low to high productivity industries with producer-goods industries expanding most rapidly, made the high overall growth rate of the economy possible.

How did the economic expansion of the Civil War affect the growth of particular industries? One of the industries hardest hit by the war had been the textile industry. But it recovered very quickly and grew at a steady rate until World War I. During that time the textile industry remained the single largest employer in the manufacturing sector. In contrast to the steady growth of textiles, "the methods of making iron and steel were being revolutionized. The iron industry was being transformed into a radically different steel industry by the impact of a new technology" (Davis et al., 1972:441). The production of pig iron, for example, increased by 7 percent annually following the Civil War, while the population grew at a rate of only 2 percent (1972:444). The growth of these industries together with machinery and coal production was undoubtedly being influenced by the rapid expansion of the railway network, which drastically reduced the cost of transportation for these commodities.

The movement of the labor force out of agriculture between 1870 and 1920 is clearly reflected in the industry composition of the labor force. In terms of absolute numbers, agriculture continued to grow until about 1910 when it reached the peak with almost 12 million persons employed (Bagwell and Mingay, 1970:85). In terms of labor force proportion, however, agricultural employment decreased rather substantially. Yet it was only after 1910 that manufacturing employed more workers than did agriculture. The most dramatic gains in employment occurred in transportation, trade, and finance, which almost doubled their labor force share between 1870 and 1920. The other remaining services did not increase at nearly the same magnitude; their labor force share grew from 12.9 to only 16.2 percent during these fifty years, which is less than 0.7 percentage points per decade. In 1920, then, the nonagricultural labor force was about equally divided between mining, manufacturing, and construction on the one hand, and the various services on the other.

As the growth of mining, manufacturing, and construction between 1910 and 1920 indicates, the economy of the United States by 1920 had again successfully achieved the transition from a wartime to a peacetime economy, and the decade of the 1920s saw a great economic expansion. The most dynamic industries during this time were building construction and the manufacture of automobiles, petroleum, radios, chemicals, and electrical equipment. "These were the industries in which technological changes combined to bring about new materials, new processes, and new products" (Peterson and Gray, 1969:384). On the other hand, the depressed industries included agriculture, coal, mining, New England textiles, and leather. Of particular importance during this time was real estate which experienced a major boom during the 1920s (Bagwell and Mingay (1970:259). But by the end of the decade, the Great Depression brought a sobering halt to economic growth. "In the two and a half years between the autumn of 1929 and the spring of 1932 the gains of the years of recovery in the 1920s were eroded in the most severe slump in world history" (Bagwell and Mingay, 1970:270).

Overall, however, the American economy in the twentieth century experienced a tremendous growth. "It has been estimated that in the late 1950's, while the United States accounted for only about 6 percent of the world's population, it produced roughly one third of the world's output" (Davis et al., 1972:59). Although the growth rate after World War I could not match that between 1860 and 1900, the performance of the economy during this time nevertheless was remarkable enough to have been called the second industrial revolution (Davis et al., 1972:464).

CANADA

Canada is one of the three countries in this study—besides Germany and Italy—that became a nation only in the last third of the nineteenth century. Initially, the three British colonies (Province of Canada, Nova Scotia, and New Brunswick) formed the Dominion of Canada in 1867. Various other colonies were included later, and Canada's present territory dates back only to 1949 when Newfoundland joined the Confederation. Although the Dominion continued to regard the English sovereign as the highest Canadian state official, in effect it became quite independent from Great Britain. Part of that growing independence is reflected in the shifts of external trade. In the nineteenth century, England was the main source of Canadian imports and the primary recipient of Canadian exports, but the direction of imports and exports moved steadily from Great Britain to the United States. By 1930, 65 percent of all Canadian imports came from the United States, and the U.S. share of total Canadian exports rose to 43 percent (Firestone, 1958: 164-65). The influence of the United States similarly is reflected in the amount of U.S. investments in Canada. By 1953 they accounted for 77.5 percent of total foreign investments as compared to the United Kingdom's share of only 17.5 percent. The growing influence of the United States has been the basis of mounting concern for Canada, for the Dominion had not achieved the termination of colonial rule in order to become subordinate to a new world power.

The outcome of this balance between the traditional ties to Great Britain and the more recent economic connections with the United States has been interpreted very differently. Easterbrook and Aitken (1956), for example, noted that, "Throughout most of its history Canada has been an economic satellite of other more advanced nations. Its exports have been almost exclusively raw materials and foodstuffs. Its imports have been manufactured goods produced by the industries of Britain and the United States. The pace of development has been set by the rise and decline of the great staple trades: fur, fish, timber, gold, wheat, and more recently pulp and paper and the base metals" (1956:515). While there exists widespread consensus among students of Canadian economic history about the importance of the staple trades for Canada's economic development, this fact has been interpreted by others in a more positive light than the interpretation given by Easterbrook and Aitken (1956). Caves and Holton (1959:43) pointed out, for example, that the staple economy required a large amount of capital, not only for transportation equipment, but also for machinery and buildings. Not only did this lay the first foundation for a banking and financing system in Canada, it also provided essential social overhead facilities to be used by other manufacturing activities. These economic forward linkages of extractive industries have propelled Canadian economic development rather than impaired it.

While the staple economy required efficient transportation, the Canadian government itself placed great emphasis on a transcontinental railway, and thus construction was undertaken with great fervor (Easterbrook and Aitken, 1956). By the end of the nineteenth century the major lines were completed, but the expansion of railways continued until 1920. From 1850 to 1920 the railway network grew at an *annual average* of 553 miles, whereas during the next thirty years only 4,174 miles were added (computed from information by Firestone, 1958:105).

As was pointed out by Caves and Holton (1959), the development of the staple economy required products from other industries such as machinery, and the manufacturing sector slowly but steadily increased its output. "From 1870 to 1890 Canadian employment in manufacturing rose by 76 percent and output in constant dollar terms 138 percent" (Firestone, 1958:207-208). During the next twenty years, from 1890 to 1910, the growth rate of manufacturing continued with the same magnitude; employment doubled and real output increased by 130 percent (Firestone, 1958:210). Most of this growth was due to the production of iron and steel, but during World War I other industries such as aircraft and shipbuilding faced increasing demands and they expanded correspondingly. Thus, by the end of the war manufacturing for the first time in Canada's history surpassed agriculture in terms of output (Easterbrook and Aitken, 1956:521).

Analyzing the development of production in the three main sectors, Firestone (1958) noted that only the decline of agriculture continued steadily, whereas the growth of manufacturing and services occurred at varying rates. "For example, around the turn of the century when mass immigration made great demands on the services industries to transport and look after the needs of millions of immigrants, and ship the greatly increased production of grain, the service sector expanded rap-

idly and manufacturing became relatively less important"
(1958:199). Secondary and tertiary industries thus alternated in
their growth, but ultimately they were to come out as the two
dominant sectors of the Canadian economy.

Evaluating Canada's economy, Firestone contended that its
growth occurred in a very balanced way. Despite the emphasis
on manufacturing expansion since the end of the nineteenth
century, the extractive sector, and forestry operations (fishing,
and mining in particular), were never neglected and maintained
an important place in the Canadian economy (1958:183). As
late as 1953 extractive industries contributed 66 percent to
total Canadian exports (1958:20). As a result of Canada's
economic efforts, each sector was able to increase its production at a faster rate than its respective labor force, although in
commercial and community services this difference is only very
slight (Lithwick, 1967:22).

In a study of the Canadian labor force, McInnis (1971) was
able to reconstruct the 1911 industry distribution of employment from previously unpublished work sheets of the Canadian
census bureau, which he then compared with the 1961 industry
structure of the labor force. McInnis' estimates are useful to
examine the employment changes during the 1911-1921 decade. The comparison of those two dates shows that the extractive and personal services sectors declined moderately, whereas
producer and distributive services expanded quite substantially.
The increase in distributive services was due mostly to transportation, which expanded from 6.9 to 8.5 percent of total
employment during the 1911-1921 decade. This increase of
employment in transportation calls into question Caves and
Holton's (1959:63) observation that the surge in the demand
for transportation during the war economy of 1914-1918 could
be handled without a significant increase in employment.

The remaining two sectors, transformative industries and
social services, about maintained their share of employment in
that decade. Despite the changes in the other industry sectors,
the most striking finding of the 1911-1921 comparison is the

similarity in the industry structure of employment in those two years; during no other decade within the 1921-1971 period did the industry structure change less than during the 1910s.

ENGLAND AND WALES

The Industrial Revolution in Britain occurred a good century and a half before the time period covered in this analysis. The first revolutionary innovations in the production of cotton were implemented in Britain in the mid-eighteenth century. As a result, "Cotton spinning was already in the factory by 1800" (Kindleberger, 1969:294), a time when countries like France and the United States had just begun their industrialization. One hundred years passed after Britain had set the example before Germany and Italy followed, and even more until Japan's transition toward a nonagricultural economy. Therefore, it is no surprise to find the British economy dominating all other countries, particularly during the first two-thirds of the nineteenth century. According to Kindleberger (1969:29), Britain reached the "apogee of its economic leadership and influence between 1850 and 1870." This was the time when Britain could rightly be called the "workshop of the world."

But despite the fact that since the middle of the nineteenth century the Industrial Revolution could no longer be described exclusively by the history of Britain, because other countries such as France or the United States were on their own ways toward industrialization, the British economy nevertheless continued to grow at a remarkable rate until the beginning of World War II.

Much of the economic growth during this time was built around four main industries: cotton, coal, iron and steel, and shipbuilding. Coal output, for example, increased about 63 million tons from 1850 to 1854 to 270 million tons during the period 1909-1913, at the same time the output of steamship building increased from 115,400 tons to 751,000 tons. "At their peak in 1913 these four industries employed some two million people, or over ten percent of the total working force" (Bagwell and Mingay, 1970:153).

In addition to the expansion of these basic industries, the British showed a great determination to save, at least until 1875. In the middle of the nineteenth century about one-sixth of the total national income was being invested (Bagwell and Mingay, 1970:7). The economically remarkable character of the time has been pointed out by Ashworth (1960:7):

> It is its astonishingly dynamic quality that is the outstanding economic characteristic of the mid-Victorian period. It was not a good time in the sense that it brought to most people a reasonable degree of stability and comfort. . . . But if the accumulation of wealth and its application to further accumulation is taken as the criterion of economic success then this was a very successful age. . . .

A third factor related to the continued economic expansion in the late nineteenth century was the growth of the labor force, which "increased by 7 million people, or 72 percent, in the second half of the nineteenth century," and its redistribution in favor of industries with a high productivity (Bagwell and Mingay, 1970:8). The growth of the labor force per se could well have presented an obstacle to economic growth (as the difficulties of many developing countries in absorbing the rapidly growing manpower demonstrate), had it not been for the expansion of the domestic market and particularly the international market. Some trade statistics illustrate Britain's comparative advantage at this time: "British exports increased in volume by 57 percent between 1871-5 and 1896-1900, and by 56 percent between 1896 and 1911-13" (Bagwell and Mingay, 1970:91).

It is somewhat of an irony, however, that in spite of this very remarkable rate of growth of the British economy during the second half of the nineteenth century, its relative position declined in comparison to other industrial countries. According to Bagwell and Mingay's statistics, for example, "Britain's share (as a proportion of world trade) fell from the 20-25 percent maintained between 1850 and 1875 to 14 percent in 1911-13" (1970:91). But considering that Britain's population in 1910 was only about forty million people, or 2.4 percent of the world population, the share of 14 percent of world trade still indicated its continuing strong economic position. The message of the declining proportion does point out, however, that Britain from now on had to compete with other nations. "Between 1890 and 1895 both the United States and Germany passed Britain in the production of steel. During the 'Great Depression' Britain ceased to be the 'workshop of the world' and merely became one of its three greatest industrial powers, and in some critical respects, the weakest of them" (Hobsbawm, 1969:127).

Various explanations have been offered for the relative decline of the British economy. Kindleberger (1969:29), for example, points out that it declined "partly because of a lack of technological capacity, but also because of the shift from coal as a source of energy to electricity and oil." The role of the technology is the most frequently cited individual factor in the discussion of Britain's changing position in the international market (e.g., Landes, 1969). In this context, Hobsbawm (1969) made some elucidating observations about the difference in the use of technology between Britain and the newer industrial countries.

> She [Britain] was too deeply committed to the technology and business organization of the first phase of industrialization, which had served her so well, to advance enthusiastically into the field of the new revolutionary technology and industrial management which came to the fore in the 1890's (1969:131).

The implications of this reluctance to make use of new technological advances were very serious indeed:

> Two major growth-industries of the new phase of industrialism, the electrical and the chemical, were entirely based on scientific knowledge. The third, the development of the internal combustion engine, though not in itself raising any scientific problems of great novelty, was dependent on at least two branches of the chemical industry: those which refined and processed the natural material of oil and rubber. . . . And by the end of the century it was already clear, espe-

cially from the experience of the German chemical industry which led the world, that the output of technological progress was a function of scientifically qualified manpower, equipment and money into systematic research projects (Hobsbawm, 1969:174).

The relative decline of the British economy ultimately resulted in the replacement of Britain by the United States as the leading industrial nation, as can be illustrated by a comparison of investments that each country channeled into the other one. "In 1914 the aggregate of British funds invested in the U.S.A. was some £800m. whilst American investment in Britain was equivalent to a mere £55m. By March 1919 British investment in the U.S.A. had shrunk to £600m whilst outstanding American loans to Britain had risen to £1,027m." (Bagwell and Mingay, 1970:240).

World War I finally revealed Britain's new economic position in the international market. Following the war Britain's immediate problem was high unemployment, which was never less than nine percent during the interwar period from 1921 to World War II (Landes, 1969:269). "Throughout the 1920's more than three-quarters of the total number of unemployed came from those industries which had flourished before 1914—coal mining, cotton textiles, shipbuilding, and iron and steel" (Bagwell and Mingay, 1970:249). The high rate of unemployment was largely the result of the failure of the new industries to absorb a sufficient number of people who left the traditional manufacturing industries. On the other hand, since Britain did not experience a boom in the 1920s as was the case in the United States or even Germany (after 1925), the impact of the World Depression on its economy was much less than in these other countries. Indeed, the 1930s were the economically more successful decade of the interwar period.

Analyzing the development of the British economy in the twentieth century, Hobsbawm (1969) noted three main tendencies: "(1) the relative decline of 'industry' as compared with tertiary employments like distribution, transport, and various services; (2) the relative decline of manual as compared with 'white-collar' or 'clean-handed' labour within each industry; (3) the decline of the characteristic nineteenth-century industries with their unusually high demand for old-fashioned manual work" (1969:285-286).

One student of the history of Germany's economic development remarked that "At the opening of the nineteenth century there was nothing that could legitimately be called a German economy" (Dillard, 1967:305). Indeed, instead of a unified country such as France or Great Britain at that time, the territory that was later to become the German *Reich* was divided into many different sovereign states with often very heterogeneous political and economic interests. Some of these states were very large and politically influential, such as Prussia, but the majority were small *Zwergstaaten.* Consequently, the transportation of goods from German ports such as Hamburg or Bremen to Berlin, for example, or from Leipzig to Munich encountered many obstacles, because numerous countries and equally numerous custom lines had to be crossed. This increased the price of goods to an extent that was prohibitive for many trading activities.

These trade barriers were dramatically changed through the creation of the *Zollverein* (Customs Union) in 1833. It has often been said that this was the first step toward the transition from an agricultural to an industrial economy in the German states and the future German *Reich* (cf., Dillard, 1967:303; Lütge, 1966:470). At the beginning of its existence, though, the *Zollverein* served agriculture and trade more than manufacturing industries, but the increasing level of trade resulting from it lead to the creation of a transportation and financial system which in turn provided the basis for the subsequent expansion of manufacturing industries. Certainly, the absence of the *Zollverein* was not the prime cause for Germany's late industrialization, and its creation was not solely responsible for its accelerated economic growth, as was pointed out by Clapham

(1936:96-101). But he, too, emphasized the great importance of that event.

From the time of the creation of the *Zollverein* to the emergence of Germany as a leading industrial nation, much had to be achieved. In 1833 Germany was predominantly an agricultural and rural country, and this changed only very slowly. From 1816 to 1871, for example, the proportion of rural population declined only slightly from 73.5 percent to 67.5 percent (Clapham, 1936:278). At the middle of the nineteenth century over one-half of the labor force worked in extractive industries, twice as much as that in transformative employment. It took two more years after the formation of the *Zollverein,* for example, until the first railroad line was opened. But once this line operated, the railway system expanded very fast. By 1865 it included 13,821 km, and it more than doubled in the following decade. It expanded to 59,031 km in 1910 (Dillard, 1967:307).

This new transportation system connected many German towns which were important for the subsequent industrial growth, because Germany's population was distributed over many small towns instead of being concentrated in a large city, such as Paris: "In 1815, what finally became the twelve largest towns of Germany, only contained between them about 50 percent more people than Paris. In 1850 the twelve towns contained 1,340,000 people and Paris more than 1,000,000" (Clapham, 1963:82). With increasing transportation facilities, more people moved to the big cities and the group of cities with more than 100,000 inhabitants increased its population share from 11.4 percent in 1890 to 21.3 percent in 1910 (Clapham, 1936:279).

Following the creation of the *Zollverein,* the period from 1850 to 1870 provided the grounds for Germany's industrial growth. Besides increasing urbanization, other factors contributed to the rapidly growing economy as well.

Forces pushing Germany toward industrialization included the railway system, the Zollverein, the growth in basic industries like mining and iron production, the formulation of joint-stock banks geared to rapid industrialization, and an aspiration for national greatness which would give Germany its rightful "place in the sun" (Dillard, 1967:307).

The second main stimulus to Germany's economic development came from its political unification in 1871. Lütge pointed to four major economic consequences that resulted from the formation of the German *Reich* (1966:470-471): (1) a national optimism that was greatly supported by the fact that Germany had just won the 1870-1871 war against France; (2) the inclusion of Alsace into the territory of the German *Reich,* which was very important to economic growth for it contained a substantial amount of coal and ferrous materials; (3) the perception among many Germans that the new nation was able to achieve political power; and finally (4) the achievement of economic unity that went well beyond the *Zollverein,* which had only abolished custom duties but which had not provided economic integration. Two other consequences of political unification should be added: the establishment of tariffs to protect the emerging industries from competition; and the early involvement of the German state in production, either through economic planning or through liberal credits to manufacturers (for an example of this interdependence between the state and the entrepreneurs in Germany, see Manchester's (1968) fascinating study of the Krupps).

It was after the foundation of the German *Reich* that industrial growth really accelerated, and in the 1880s the first comparisons were being made between English and German manufacturing of iron and steel (Clapham, 1936:283-285). Other industries related to the rapid economic expansion included chemical products and machinery, particularly electrical machinery. In contrast, the textile industry never achieved the importance that it had in England or France (Dillard, 1967:313).

From the beginning of German industrialization the leading industries in Germany belonged to the modern sector of manufacturing, which refers to the manufacturing of chemicals and electrical machinery in particular (Lütge, 1966:417-418). Here, Germany did not have to catch up with any other nation but could be among the leaders from the very outset. The development of chemical production in particular helped Germany build a dynamic manufacturing sector. Besides providing a number of new fertilizers, which resulted in increasing the productivity of agriculture, many chemical products, such as pharmaceutical goods and dyestuffs, could be exported. All these developments contributed to the formation of capital which was badly needed for investments in the rapidly expanding manufacturing sector (Dillard, 1967:309; Clapham, 1936:303-309).

Besides chemicals, electrical machinery proved to be a key industry for Germany's efforts to industrialize: "Next to chemical industries, it offered the greatest outlet for the scientific and organizational best of the Germans" (Dillard, 1967:213). Dominated by two gigantic firms (Siemens and A.E.G.) this industry had developed, in a very short time, from a small handicraft operation to a world enterprise. Part of this development is reflected in the census: in 1882 no special category was provided for electrical machinery, but by 1895, 26,000 people were employed in these industries. Ten years later A.E.G. alone employed 31,000 people out of a total of 109,000 working in electrical machinery (Clapham, 1966:308).

Given the new electrical and chemical technology, it was only a short step to make Germany one of the leading steel producers, because the process of steel production is based on the combined expertise of chemistry and metallurgy, and by 1910 Germany's steel and iron production surpassed that of Great Britain.

According to Clapham, "The period 1890-1910 is shown to have been that in which Germany took the lead in Europe, with a speed and decision which confirmed the most confident faith of her people in their industrial and political future" (1936:885). By now Germany's external trade was well established and its revenues from the export of chemical and electrical goods provided it with enough capital to continue this expansion of the manufacturing sector.

This growing prosperity came to an end, however, with the outbreak of World War I. As a result of Germany's defeat, the *Reich* lost 13 percent of its territory, which contained 15 percent of the total cultivatible land, 75 percent of all ferrous mineral resources, and 26 percent of all coal reserves (Lütge, 1966:339). In addition, one of the bases of the economy, external trade, was severely restricted and many foreign markets were closed to German goods. Although by 1926 the prewar volume of external trade was reached again, the new momentum was stopped by the world economic crisis in the late 1920s. According to Lütge (1966:550), German exports decreased from 13.5 million to 4.8 million Reichsmark during the 1929-1932 period.

After 1933, the character of the economy was pronouncedly changed by the war preparations of the Nazis. One result of this was an increase in the manufacture of machinery and transportation equipment. Also, construction employment rose as a result of Hitler's plans to build a strategic network of interstate highways (Autobahn) as part of his war preparations.

While most of Germany had been in no direct contact with war activities during World War I, the opposite was true for World War II. By 1945, the German territory as well as its economy were in shambles. Thus, much of the economic activities in the 1950s must be seen in the context of reconstruction, which is reflected by an extremely large volume of construction activities and by an above average growth rate in production and national income.

FRANCE

It has been said that the French economy is characterized by two features: its domination by agriculture, and a high proportion of small businesses (Meiklereid, 1953:1). While this description sought to portray the France of 1952, these two features were even more important in earlier decades. Why is it that the French economy grew at a much slower rate than those of its neighbors, although France started its industrialization a decade earlier than, say, Germany (Bairoch, 1971)? Some of the factors

have been isolated by Clough (1946), and he refers to the
following weak segments of the French economy:

> Apparently, French income from commerce, transportation, public
> administration, and domestic, personal, and professional services was
> excessively low in comparison with the countries of large income per
> capita. Income from agriculture was also low, the value of net
> agricultural output in France having declined in the twentieth cen-
> tury. And although the index of French manufacturing was in 1938
> about twice that in 1900, France produced in the years 1926-1929
> factory goods, exclusive of foodstuffs, to the value of $96 per capita
> of the population at the prevailing prices, while Germany produced
> factory goods to the value of $111 per capita, and the United
> Kingdom to the value of $112 per capita (1946:94).

Clough concluded that from the very beginning France did not
have many competitive advantages in manufacturing, hardly any
in agriculture, and "decided disadvantages in commerce, transport, and services" (1946:94).

Much has been made of the fact that France lacked available
natural resources such as coal. (Habakkuk, 1955: Bettelheim,
1947; Walter, 1957; Clough, 1946). But Kindleberger (1964)
pointed out that this would be akin to stating that the British
economy was disadvantaged because of its lack of cotton.
Rather, the important question, according to Kindleberger, is the
cost of coal or of any other energy resource, "and this turns on
location, transport, and tariff policy" (1964:18). While this is
not the place to decide the issue of natural resources, Kindleberger's point is an interesting one because it relates to the
question as to whether or not employment in a given industry,
such as transportation, is vital for the growth of employment in
another industry. In the case of France, however, a special
situation exists. On the one hand its road network is the densest
in Europe (Thompson, 1970:108) and it has an equally dense
railroad system (Meiklereid, 1953). On the other, the organization of the transportation system has been mainly shaped by
economic forces whose interests centered around Paris with its
political influence and financial facilities. As a result, much of

France's transportation system reinforced the already present centralization tendencies of the economy as well as the population (Hansen, 1970).

> The deliberate focusing of 'routes nationales' on Paris, from the sixteenth century onwards, has left lacunae in the network in terms of inter-regional links. This is particularly the case in the western half of the nations, where the lack of heavy industry excluded the play of economic forces sufficiently strong to overcome the political forces of centralization. Although a remodelling of the basic network is not feasible, a priority need is to improve the capacity of the existing interregional connections both within western France and transversally to the Mediterranean and the north. Such improvements would integrate the major ports of the west more effectively with their hinterlands and create situations for new industries that would have access to the major urban markets of eastern France (Thompson, 1970:109).

The most important consequence of this insufficient transportation network was the fact that the imported coal could only be transported from the western ports at a very high cost, which made the overall price of coal almost prohibitive. Similarly, agricultural products could not be transported efficiently enough for exports which could have given France part of its badly needed capital for sustained economic growth. The interplay of all these factors resulted in a situation where France fell more and more behind Britain and Germany in the late mineteenth century.

Despite the slower overall growth of the economy, it nevertheless can be divided into periods of acceleration and retardation. The latest period of economic acceleration before 1920 was 1896-1913, and steel, automobiles, electricity, and chemicals were the leading industries in that time. Starting in the early 1920s another economic acceleration began, and this time chemicals led the way (Perroux, 1955; Rostow, 1960). The importance of the chemical industry has been questioned, however, by Kindleberger who showed that its production fell much behind that of Germany and Switzerland (1964: 298-300). According to him, the automobile industry was more important

during that time, mainly because of its heavy export orientation. "Half of the French automobile output, in fact, was
exported, and half of this to Britain" (Kindleberger 1964:300).

Despite the heavy losses in World War I, the French industrializing performance during the 1920s compare favorably with
that of other countries, such as Great Britain (Ogburn and Jaffe,
1929). In the 1930s, however, the rapid pace of industrialization slowed down decidedly, and it was not until the 1950s that
the French economy recovered.

ITALY

Not until 1861 was Italy formed as a politically, economically, and administratively unified country. In contrast to other
countries, such as Great Britain or France with their centralized
administrations that had been established much earlier, for a
long time Italy was faced with a confusing system of trade
barriers which posed a serious obstacle to its industrialization
(see Clough, 1964:28-56 for a discussion of the relationship
between Italy's political unification and its economic development. It is not surprising to find that the 1861 census reported
71 percent of the population to be illiterate. This was in part
related to the fact that Italy at the time of unification was
primarily rural, with over half of the population pursuing agricultural activities that accounted for about 60 percent of national production. In contrast, industry "produced less than a
fifth of the national output and was often extremely weak since
it had developed artificially under the shelter of the protective
customs policies of the preexisting small states" (Aggradi, 1961:
88).

While the scope of this study does not permit an extensive
investigation of regional differences within a country in terms
of economic diversification, in the case of Italy it nevertheless
must be pointed out that we are dealing with a truly dual
economy. Much has been said about this situation (e.g. Lutz,
1962), for the economic structures of the North and the South
are as different as could be found in a comparison of an
industrially advanced country with a developing one. On the

other hand, however, national economic policies do affect both parts of the country, such as the exchange of labor, although it is recognized that in most cases the North benefitted from economic growth at the expense of the South. But recently, great efforts have been made to shift centers of industrial growth to the South (Sundquist, 1974), and it is therefore meaningful for our purposes to analyze Italy's national economy rather than its regions.

As was the case in all industrialized countries (see e.g., Cochran and Thomas, 1968), the expansion of railways was one of the most stimulating factors for Italy's economic growth. "Building railway networks meant that a great labor force was employed for money wages and that workers became accustomed to going to the market for their purchases" (Clough, 1964:23). Besides employing people, railway construction led to the formation of new enterprises, which, in turn, created capital, issued stocks, and to a large extent provided the basis for a modern banking and finance system.

While the railway system had already expanded heavily between 1848 and 1861 (Clough, 1964:23-26), its size remained very small in 1861, with only 1,623 miles of railways. Dividing the railway network into North and South highlights the vast differences between the two regions: Of the total network, only 78 miles were in the South (Aggradi, 1961:289). Although working with slightly different figures, Clough (1964:66) comes to a similar conclusion.

After the unification, however, railway construction accelerated at a very fast pace. According to Clough (1964:66), the railway network increased from 1,623 miles in 1861 to 16,053 miles in 1896, with the major national transportation lines being completed at that time. Thus, within 35 years, the railway network increased by almost 1,000 percent.

Despite this rapid progress in the transportation system, Italy's economic growth was retarded by a number of obstacles, primarily the problem of raising capital. On the one hand, agriculture did not produce efficiently enough to generate surplus capital which could have been invested in industries of capital goods and consumption goods. Capital was badly needed because the economy had to depend on imports of many raw products which could not be found in Italy. For these reasons, the state assumed a large role in the acceleration of economic growth by subsidizing large industries such as shipbuilding, and some of these involvements (in banking, for example) have been maintained until the present day.

But, of course, Italy's economy did grow stronger, particularly after 1897 (Aggradi, 1961:294), and its leading sectors were the following: "Among the major components of its national economic infrastructure were railways, an iron and steel industry, a merchant marine and shipbuilding plants, and a banking system which could foster savings for investments" (Clough, 1964:60). While the growth of textile industries was very remarkable (their production increased from 12,400 tons in 1861 to 201,900 tons in 1913 (Clough, 1964:62), the largest increase in production occurred in metal and machinery production. "By 1914, the metallurgical and machine trades together were more important, measured by value added, than any other single branch of economy" (Clough, 1964:82).

One of the best indicators of economic growth is the production of energy, and the expanding economic activities that were discussed in the previous paragraphs are clearly reflected by the volume of generated energy. While the annual average of energy production in the 1881-1891 decade was only 3 million kilowatt-hours, this increased to 3,192 million in the 1911-1920 decade (Clough, 1964:97).

Thus, by 1920 Italy clearly had passed its first stages of economic growth and was on the way toward the formation of a strong manufacturing sector.

JAPAN

Despite the many differences between the various countries that have been discussed so far in this chapter, to some extent they share a common historical experience, which in the case of Canada and the United States, stems from the large flow of European immigrants. This is not true in the case of Japan, and it would take a separate chapter to discuss the many ways in which the differences between Japan and the other six countries manifest themselves. One may think, for example, of the contrasting forms of organization in factories (cf. Dore, 1973; Cole, 1971), different labor relations (Cole, 1973), or general societal differences (Nakane, 1972). As Irene Taeuber (1957:91) put it: "Japan's economic transformation is difficult to describe in numerical terms because it involved an integration of things Western and things Eastern." Yet, as has been mentioned earlier in this study, the present focus on changes in the industry structure of the labor force does not require a comprehensive discussion of all dimensions of economic development. As will be seen in the analysis of Japan's labor force, its changes over time are remarkable enough to merit attention independently. In that sense, the inclusion of Japan with this study serves as a contrast to the experience of Britain. In the case of the latter. the sectoral transformation of the labor force was examined in the absence of a substantial share of employment in the extractive sector, whereas the Japanese case serves as an illustration of a situation in which over one half of the total labor force is engaged in agriculture. But again, caution is called for in generalizing from the Japanese case:

> As an object lesson with specific application to development countries, the Japanese experience is probably of limited value, for at least two obvious reasons. First, the historical period during which Japan industrialized had unique characteristics which can never be repeated for the benefit of presently industrializing countries. Second, the unusual racial homogeneity and sense of nationhood among the Japanese is rarely found in developing nations (Cole, 1971:11).

The examination of labor force changes in Japan, therefore, should be seen as a further example for the contention made earlier that countries have to follow their own patterns of economic transformation.

Unfortunately, our knowledge of the labor force in the last century and the first two decades of this century is solely based on estimates, because the first Japanese population census was taken in 1920. Given the customary cautions in dealing with demographic estimates, the data in Table 2.1 nevertheless do indicate some broad trends. Within a time-span of only 35 years, primary employment (and particularly agriculture) declined from over 80 percent of total employment to under 60 percent, while both secondary and tertiary employment increased during this period. It is noteworthy that according to this data, tertiary employment has always been significantly larger than secondary employment, although around 1915 the gap had been somewhat narrowed. But what do these labor force data reflect? In order to place these data and the analysis of the period 1920-1970 in the larger framework of Japan's economic growth, some general orientation is provided here concerning Japan's economic and demographic structure and its relation to the international market.

The year 1868 is considered the beginning of Japan's industrialization. On that date the *Shogunate* fell and a new structure of national administration and taxation was created that laid the foundations for the emergence of Japan as a leading industrial nation (Lockwood, 1968: 8). One of the first steps taken by this administration concerned the trade with other nations. Two major developments resulted from Japan's turn toward the international community. First, a substantial share of foreign imports was made up by investment goods (mainly from Great Britain) which greatly accelerated the growth of the Japanese manufacturing sector. Second, the most important result of the increasing volume of foreign trade was the recognition of the

Table 2.1: Estimated Labor Force Distribution by Industry Sectors: Japan, Selected Years (in percentages)

Year	Primary Sector	Secondary Sector	Tertiary Sector	
1878-1882	82.3	5.6	12.1	(100.0)
1898-1902	69.9	11.8	18.3	(100.0)
1913-1917	59.2	16.4	24.4	(100.0)

Source: Ohkawa (1957)

necessity to build a transportation and communication system, both internally and internationally. The government was among the first to realize that need and it invested large amounts of capital into the construction of railways, highways, communication lines, and steam vessels. While the function of external trade will be discussed later in much more detail it is noted here in passing that external trade played a significant role in Japan's economic growth. Certainly, it was not a new development after World War II, although its dimension then increased at an unprecedented rate.

If 1868 marked the year of Japan's beginning Industrial Revolution, the end of the nineteenth century can be called the turning point of the new industrial economy.

> The assimilation of machine technology, the accumulation of banking and industrial capital, the expansive influences of world prosperity and rising prices—all facilitated a rapid rise of industrial output. Especially was this true for textiles and other consumer goods. Two victorious wars, at an interval of a decade, gave additional impetus to the development of transport, banking, and strategic industries under the leadership of the State and the nacent *zia bat su*. By 1914 Japanese industrial capitalism was still weak and rudimentary by comparison with the advanced economies of the West. But it had now emerged from its formative stage. The basic patterns were established which were to characterize it for the next quarter century (Lockwood, 1968:18).

Among the changes that had to occur before Japan could reach its dominant economic position of today, was the need for a modern bureaucracy and economies of scale, a larger urban population, and a skilled labor force that would be capable of meeting the new technological demands. For as late as 1920, the Japanese economy was clearly dominated by agriculture, at least as far as the labor force is concerned.

International Events, 1920-1970

Although the seven countries included in this study had their own specific problems in the transition from an agricultural to

an industrial (and later postindustrial) economy, the time period covered in this study includes several important international events that affected the countries in a similar way. Of
these events, the three economically most important ones were
the consequences of World War I, the World Depression in the
late 1920s, and the outbreak of World War II. The impact of
these events on the economies of the selected countries, as well
as on the structure of the international market, was so great
that they merit a separate discussion before moving to an
examination of the national labor force trends.

In the period following World War I most national economies
experienced an increasing economic growth rate, which was
partly reflected in the accelerated decline of agricultural employment and the continuing shift of the labor force toward
transformative and service industries. For some countries, however, the outcome of the war had quite different consequences.
It had been widely acknowledged, for example, that the Canadian economy was stimulated by both world wars (Caves and
Holton, 1959). On the other hand, Germany's loss of World War
I and the subsequent Treaty of Versailles resulted in many
economic obligations on its part that made economic recovery
extremely difficult. Only after the years of heavy inflation
during the early 1920s was Germany able to continue her
economic growth at a rate comparable to the prewar period.
While Germany at least was spared physical destruction during
the war, France suffered more and was pushed backwards in
terms of modernizing its economy, despite the reparations received from Germany.

The industry structure of the labor force as reported by the
1920 censuses, therefore, has to be evaluated in part as being
influenced by World War I and in part as already reflecting the
new era of economic expansion and prosperity for which the
1920s earned their fame. But this prosperity was not to last
very long.

At the end of the 1920s the World Depression put a momentary but drastic halt to economic growth in all seven countries of this study. This crisis had truly international dimensions: "Between 1929 and 1932 the value of world trade

declined by nearly two-thirds and its volume by one-third" (Bagwell and Mingay, 1970:270). In the absence of employment opportunities in transformative industries, agricultural manpower remained on the land. As a result, the flow of employment from extractive to transformative and services industries diminished. For these reasons, transformative employment in 1930 remained at about the 1920 level or even declined in most countries. Only social services (and to a lesser extent personal services) were less influenced by the World Depression.

After the early 1930s, however, the economies of all countries under consideration began to recover and they continued to flourish until the outbreak of World War II. Because of the war, the 1940 census is available only for the three non-European countries, i.e., the United States, Canada, and Japan. These existing censuses clearly demonstrate the recovery of the three economies from the World Depression. The data reveal that the Canadian as well as the United States economy had become predominantly nonagricultural, and that Japan also had moved in that direction at a rapid pace. Although 1940 census data do not exist for the European countries, employment data collected during the 1930s in these countries show that their labor force trends were consistent with those of the other three countries. The transformative sector in particular is likely to have expanded during the war, since the demand in these times was mainly for manufactured goods. A similar demand existed for transportation services but in this industry it could more easily be met with the already existing manpower or with only a slight increase.

The end of World War II brought great changes to the international scene. The United States clearly emerged as the leading nation of the West, dominating capitalist Europe for the following decades. Canada, too, came out of the war with a strengthened economy, but its size did not permit international leadership.

On the other hand, the war was devastating for all European economies, regardless of the side they were on, and Japan's economy was equally paralyzed. Providing housing was a primary necessity in the postwar period. Since many bridges, roads, railways, and factories had to be reconstructed as well, a very large proportion of the gross national products was invested in construction. Therefore, it is not very surprising to find that the employment share of construction reached the highest level in 1950 and 1960 for the European countries and Japan.

In contrast, the manufacturing industries were severely impaired by the war and by the small amount of capital available, at least until 1950. The employment shares of these industries therefore remained low and declined in many cases. It was primarily during the 1950s that the manufacturing sector experienced a new upswing and output in 1960 reached an all-time high.

As was the case during the World Depression, service activities, and social services in particular, were much less influenced by the consequences of the war, and their employment share continued to expand. In fact, social services are the only sector in some countries which increased their employment share between 1940 and 1950.

The 1950s and 1960s finally presented a similar situation for all countries of this study in that the national economies experienced a remarkable growth rate. As a result, the employment share of agriculture continued to decline at an accelerated pace, and transformative industries, and social and producer services proved to be the most dynamic sectors during the decade.

Besides illustrating the common way in which the various national economies responded to the main international events during the 1920-1960 period, the preceding discussion points to some important methodological considerations. The practice of most countries to take a census every ten years (with the exception of France, where the interval between censuses has been eight years after World War II) limits the utility of these data for this study considerably. Both the 1930 and the 1940 census were taken at a rather extraordinary time (if any time in history can be called ordinary). For instance, it can be expected that if in a particular country a census had been taken in 1928 it would have revealed a very different distribution of the labor force by industries than that reported by the 1930 census, the reason for this, of course, being the World Depression. To the extent that the World Depression was an uncommon event, the 1930 labor force distribution was uncommon as well, at least in comparison to the overall trend of the sectoral transformation of the labor force. A similar difference would be expected between the industry structure in 1940 and that in early 1939, before World War II broke out. On the other hand, these events form part of the experience of the industrialized countries that are considered in this study, and their analysis is interesting in itself. How did the various countries react to these obstacles to economic growth? What were the consequences for their sectoral transformation of the labor force? The second question in particular is of great importance for the following analysis of national labor force trends. These considerations indicate, once again, that the experience of the advanced industrialized countries cannot serve as blueprints for the transformation of the labor force in currently developing countries. In the present analysis, then, it must be realized that each point in time of enumeration is somewhat arbitrary. A census in 1925 would probably reflect the high rate of economic expansion that existed in most countries during the 1920s, but it would at the same time ignore the difficulties countries had to face at the end of that decade. In the ideal case, a study of the labor force transformation would be based on yearly data, but decennial censuses are the only sources which permit sufficient differentiation of the labor force. But undoubtedly the census dates will have to be seen in close relation to the various historical events occurring at the respective time.

Before moving to the main purpose of this study which is the analysis of the sectoral transformation of the labor force during the past fifty years, mention should be made of the terminology used throughout the remainder of the analysis to describe labor force changes. At this time, attention is being paid only to changes in the *distribution* of the labor force by industries in *proportionate* (percentage) terms. It therefore should be kept in mind that the characterization of an industry as "increasing" or "decreasing" refers only to changes in their employment share of the total labor force. It may well be that in many cases the proportion of the labor force in a particular industry declines although its absolute level of employment continues to grow. This simply indicates that the growth rate of that particular industry is smaller than the growth rate of the total labor force. Generally, given the existing rate of population growth in the countries of this study and the related growth rate of the labor force, a specific industry must show a very substantial *proportionate* employment decline in order to decline in absolute numbers as well. With this in mind, we will now turn to the analysis of the sectoral transformation of the labor force in North America, Western Europe, and Japan.

Chapter 3

LABOR FORCE TRENDS: INTERNATIONAL PERSPECTIVES

The industry structure of employment in industrialized countries underwent a sweeping transformation during the past 50 years. The changes entailed in this transformation are so numerous that one could easily drown in the detail of information. For that reason, the following decisions were made for the presentation of the findings. First, the transformation of employment will be discussed on the level of industry sectors. It was found that these sectors capture most of the employment changes. Where more specific information is warranted, detailed industries will be introduced, such as construction, transportation, trade, and domestic service. (Those readers that have a special interest in one of the seven countries are referred to Appendix A and to the lengthy discussion of these countries in Singelmann, 1974:65-171.) Second, in the light of the concern with services, the internal structure of the traditional tertiary sector and its changes will receive special attention.

The Total Labor Force

EXTRACTIVE SECTOR

Consistent with the anticipations formulated in Chapter 1, the employment share of the extractive sector decreased con-

Table 3.1: Percentage Distribution of Employment by Industry Sectors: Seven Industrialized Countries, 1920-1970

Sectors and Countries	About 1920	About 1930	About 1940	About 1950	About 1960	About 1970
Extractive						
United States	28.9	25.4	21.3	14.4	8.1	4.5
Canada	36.9	34.4	31.7	21.6	14.7	9.1
England	14.2	11.8	a	8.9	6.6	4.2
Germany	33.5	31.5	a	16.1	9.0	5.1
France	43.6	38.3	40.2	31.9	23.0	17.0
Italy	57.1	48.1	a	42.9	29.8	b
Japan	56.3	50.9	46.3	50.3	34.1	20.0
Transformative						
United States	32.9	31.5	29.8	33.9	35.9	33.9
Canada	26.1	24.7	28.2	33.7	31.2	30.0
England	42.2	39.3	a	45.4	46.0	43.8
Germany	38.9	38.3	a	47.3	51.3	49.0
France	29.7	32.8	29.6	35.2	37.7	39.3
Italy	24.2	29.2	a	32.0	40.0	b
Japan	19.8	19.8	24.9	21.0	28.5	34.3
Distributive Services						
United States	18.7	19.6	20.4	22.4	21.9	22.1
Canada	19.2	18.4	17.6	21.7	23.9	23.0
England	19.3	21.6	a	19.2	19.7	17.9
Germany	11.9	12.8	a	15.7	16.4	16.9
France	14.4	13.3	15.1	14.4	16.4	15.5
Italy	8.6	10.1	a	10.6	13.1	b
Japan	12.5	15.6	15.2	14.6	18.6	22.7
Producer Services						
United States	2.8	3.2	4.6	4.8	6.6	9.3
Canada	3.7	3.3	2.8	4.0	5.3	7.3
England	2.6	3.1	a	3.2	4.5	5.6
Germany	2.1	2.7	a	2.5	4.2	5.1
France	1.6	2.1	1.9	2.7	3.2	5.5
Italy	1.3	1.8	a	1.9	2.0	b
Japan	0.8	0.9	1.2	1.5	2.9	5.1
Social Services						
United States	8.7	9.2	10.0	12.4	16.3	21.5
Canada	7.5	8.9	9.4	11.3	15.3	21.1
England	8.9	9.7	a	12.1	14.1	19.4
Germany	6.0	6.8	a	11.5	12.9	17.4
France	5.3	6.1	6.8	9.4	12.3	14.8
Italy	4.1	5.2	a	7.9	9.4	b
Japan	4.9	5.5	6.0	7.2	8.3	10.2
Personal Services						
United States	8.2	11.2	14.0	12.1	11.3	8.6
Canada	6.7	10.3	10.3	7.8	9.6	9.5
England	12.9	14.5	a	11.3	9.0	9.0

Table 3.1: (Cont'd)

Sectors and Countries	About 1920	About 1930	About 1940	About 1950	About 1960	About 1970
Germany	7.7	7.8	a	6.8	6.4	6.5
France	5.6	7.2	6.4	7.4	7.4	7.9
Italy	4.6	5,6	a	4.7	5,9	b
Japan	5.7	7.3	6.3	5.3	7.6	7.6

a. The European countries did not take a census during World War II (the French census was taken in 1946).
b. At the time of this writing, the data for Italy are not yet available.
Source: See Appendix A.

tinuously in all countries during each decade (see Table 3.1). The only two exceptions are France where the employment share of this sector increased between 1931 and 1946, and Japan between 1940 and 1950. Both instances, however, can be explained by the impact of World War II. Only one year after the end of the war, economic activities in France still suffered from the extensive destruction of production facilities, and it should, therefore, not be surprising to find that the share of the labor force in the extractive sector in 1946 was 1.9 percentage points higher than it was in 1931. Similar conditions existed in Japan at that time when the extractive sector increased its share of the labor force from 46.3 to 50.3 percent between 1940 and 1950. Given the remarkable decline of the extractive sector in the following decade in both countries, the overall pattern of declining extractive employment is not invalidated by these two exceptions.

The dimensions of this sectoral transformation is revealed by examining the diminishing size of this sector during the five decades. In 1920, the share of employment in the extractive sector accounted for over one-third of the labor force in five countries, and even ten years later no country, with the sole exception of England, had less than one-fourth of its total labor force in extractive activities. By 1970, however, no country had more than one-fifth of its total employment in this sector, and that proportion had dropped to below ten percent in England, the United States, Germany, and Canada.

TRANSFORMATIVE SECTOR

In contrast to the dramatic decline of the extractive sector, transformative industries increased their share of the labor force between 1920 and 1970 in all countries. But this growth was not continuous throughout the fifty year period, because the world economic crisis of 1929 and the outbreak of the Second World War imposed great strains on the national economies. With the end of World War II, however, the transformative sector entered the period of its greatest expansion which lasted until 1960. The only country in which transformative employment declined in the 1950s is Canada.

For most countries, 1960 is the year in which the transformative share reached its largest proportion of total employment in this 50 year period (the exceptions to this situation are Japan and France); it subsequently declined during the 1960s in the United States, Canada, England, and Germany.

This decline is not surprising in the case of Germany and England. Both countries had such a dominating sector that a further expansion would have been difficult. Yet even by 1970, these two countries have relatively more employment in transformative industries than any other country during the 1920-1970 period.

But the decline of the transformative sector between 1960 and 1970 in the United States and Canada is more important. It confirms what the earlier decline in Canada during the 1950s had already suggested: transformative employment (as a proportion of total employment) reached its zenith at a much lower level than in the case of the European countries. (In that sense, the continued expansion of the transformative sector in France during the 1960s is consistent with the experience of Germany and England.) The transformative sector is clearly the dominant sector in the four European countries, and both England and Germany already had a larger share of their labor forces in transformative industries in 1920 than was ever reached by Canada or the United States. In the two North American countries, the transformative sector expanded to about one-third of total employment, whereas it accounts for 40 percent or more in the European countries.

In the case of Japan, the low 28.5 percent employed in transformative industries seems surprising at first, but it should be remembered that Japan's expansion of its exports occurred primarily after 1960. It was only around 1958-1959 that the volume of Japanese exports regained the 1934-1936 level, but by 1963 it was almost twice that size (Lockwood, 1968: 595). The data for 1970 clearly show the expansion of transformative industries as a result of these gains of exports. But given today's position of Japan as one of the leading export nations of the world, its transformative sector still appears relatively small compared with Germany and England. Different technology and product-mix have made it possible for Japan to produce a high volume of manufacturing output with a moderate size of employment in these industries. Therefore, one might expect that the future employment trend of the transformative sector in Japan will follow more the North American pattern than the European one.

It was noted earlier in the discussion of sector allocation schemes (see Chapter 2) that the proportion employed in construction is large enough to permit its classification as a separate sector. This is supported by the data in Table 3.2. Indeed, employment in construction has always been substantially

Table 3.2: Employment in Construction as Proportion of Total Labor Force: Seven Industrialized Countries, 1920-1970

Country	About 1920	About 1930	About 1950	About 1960	About 1970
United States	a	6.5	6.2	6.2	5.8
Canada	9.0	6.8	6.9	7.0	6.9
England	4.4	5.2	6.5	6.9	7.1
Germany	5.3	6.1	9.3	8.5	8.0
France	3.0	4.2	7.4	8.7	10.3
Italy	4.0	6.0	7.6	12.0	a
Japan	2.7	3.3	4.3	6.2	7.6

a. No data available
Source: See Appendix A.

larger than the total producer services sector (with the only exceptions of the United States in 1960 and 1970, and Canada in 1970). But the more important finding of Table 3.2 is that even when construction was taken out of the transformative sector, it would not fundamentally alter the previous conclusion that European countries employ more people in manufacturing than their North American counterparts.

DISTRIBUTIVE SERVICES SECTOR

The employment changes in distributive services resemble those of the transformative sector very closely. Overall, the share of employment in this sector increased in all countries; thus, the 1970 shares are larger than the 1920 shares, with the only exception of England. It must be noted, however, that distributive services lost proportionate employment at various times in most of the seven countries; only in Germany and Italy did their relative employment increase continuously. Most of the decreases occurred during the 1930-1950 period, and Canada was the only country to show a declining share of employment in distributive services in the 1920s.

Turning attention to the changes in distributive services employment after 1950, it can be seen that the countries with the smallest employment shares in 1950—France, Italy, and Japan—accounted for the largest increase during the 1950s. By 1970, the North American countries and Japan had around 22-23 percent of employment in this sector, with a corresponding percentage of 15-18 for the European countries.

In order to comprehend the employment changes in the distributive sector, a differentiation between transportation and trade is necessary (communication is too small, in terms of employment, to make any difference one way or the other). The development of transportation and trade took two different turns. From 1920 to 1970, relative employment in transportation declined steadily and reached a level of 4-5.5 percent in the seven countries (see the tables in Appendix A). The exceptions to this trend are Italy and Japan; their transportation industries were the smallest in 1920 and the subsequent devel-

Table 3.3: Employment in Trade as Proportion of Total Labor Force: Seven Industrialized Countries, 1920-1970

Country	1920	1930	1950	1960	1970
United States	11.1	12.6	15.8	16.1	16.9
Canada	10.7	10.3	13.9	15.2	15.5
England	12.0	14.6	12.8	14.0	13.0
Germany	7.9	8.6	10.6	11.4	13.0
France	8.1	8.5	8.8	10.5	11.1
Italy	4.3	5.4	6.6	8.1	a
Japan	8.5	11.6	10.1	13.6	16.3

a. No data available.
Source: See Appendix A.

opment during the fifty-year period brought them into line with the other countries.

Two reasons can be given for the decline of transportation. First, the past fifty years brought with them a drastic change in the nature of transportation. It was during this time that the automobile became the favorite mode of getting from one place to another. As a result, the transportation of persons by public means became less important. Second, once a comprehensive transportation network is created—this is particularly true for railroads—it is capable of handling large increases in demand without corresponding increases in employment. This is to a large extent the result of technological advances which permit various economics and, thereby, increasing productivity many times (see Cottrell's article, 1951, *Death by Dieselization*, as a good example for the influence of technology on transportation).

In contrast to the overall decline of transportation, trade expanded its share of total employment throughout the fifty years in all countries. Moreover, whereas transportation accounted for very similar shares of employment in the seven countries, there is much more variation among them for trade (see Table 3.3). Again, the North American countries, including Japan, have a much higher share of employment in trade than is the case for the European countries. These differences must largely be attributed to retail trade rather than wholesale trade. For the European countries, England in 1970 had the highest share with 9.6 percent in retailing, whereas the corresponding figures for the United States and Canada are 12.8 and 11.0, respectively. (Japan's share of 10.2 percent in retailing, whereas the corresponding figures for the United States and Canada are 12.8 and 11.0, respectively. (Japan's share of 10.2 percent in retailing shows that in this case, a large wholesale industry contributed to the high overall figure for trade.)

These findings come as a surprise, for the opposite situation should have been expected. There seems to be little doubt that the supermarket concept of retailing is the more efficient form of organization than the little store "around the corner" which is so typical for European countries. (Despite a trend toward self-service establishments in Europe after the war, small stores there are still more prevalent than in the United States.) And indeed, supermarkets are beginning to gain ground, even in France and Italy. Why, then, does retailing absorb a higher proportion of the labor force in North America than in Europe? While part of the answer may be related to the possibility that North Americans consume more than Europeans and thus require more retail employment per capita, it is believed that the main reason for the differences is the quality of service offered.

In Europe, the opening hours of retail establishments are much shorter than in North America. In Germany and France, stores normally close around 6:00 or 7:00 p.m., and where they remain open longer in the evening such as in Southern France or Italy, they commonly close for a siesta during the day. On a Saturday, the opening hours are even shorter and often restricted to the morning and early afternoon. Given this schedule, European retail stores generally operate with a one-shift labor force.

The reasons for the limited opening schedule of most European retail establishments are not entirely clear. In most European countries, store hours are regulated by the state. Despite periodic pressures by consumer oriented groups to extend the opening hours in order to enable the working population to shop more price consciously by comparing sale offers, labor unions and the association of independent retailers have consistently opposed such extension, although for different reasons. The unions have argued that such a step could potentially lead to an exploitation of retail clerks by forcing them to work longer hours than the regular work week. So far, they have not accepted the argument that longer store hours could be beneficial for labor because it would create new employment opportunities. But with drastically increased unemployment during the 1970s even in West Germany, labor unions might soften their opposition to an extension of store hours. The independent retailers, on the other hand, oppose the extension because they fear that the higher labor costs of that extension would make it even more difficult for them to compete with the large retail chains.

In contrast, store hours in the United States are much longer, and a 9:00 a.m. to 9:00 p.m. schedule Monday through Saturday is not uncommon. This forces most retail stores to operate on a two-shift schedule. In addition, many food stores in the United States are open on Sundays, and since the 1950s the concept of the twenty-four hour convenience stores has become widespread. Again, none of this exists in Europe. Other labor intensive services include the bagging of food by special employees which is often found in the United States, while these services have to be performed by the customer in Europe.

Thus, the differences between the North American and the European countries in the proportion of employment allocated to retail trade are the result of several factors. Two of them are the different store hours and the differential quality in the service that is offered to the customer. Other factors that would need to be examined include the volume of sales in the two groups of countries. If it could be shown that the longer opening hours result in higher amount of sales, attention could then be focussed on the volume of sales rather than on the length of store hours. Finally, to fully evaluate the proportion of employment in retailing in the various countries, the product mix of sales must be examined. It might well be that although the per capita amount of sales is the same in Europe as in North America, Europeans purchase, on the average, more expensive goods than Americans. Since a higher value of the average sales transaction would reduce the requirement for labor in retailing, such a finding could, in part, explain the differences in the level of retail employment between Europe and North America.

PRODUCER SERVICES SECTOR

Although producer services make up the smallest sector of the labor force, they nevertheless have shown a very remarkable increase since 1920 in all seven countries. In relative terms, this sector did decline in some countries during the 1920s and the 1930s, but since 1940 employment in producer services has continuously expanded in every country. The dynamics of this sector is demonstrated by the fact that its share of employment doubled from 1920 to 1970 in all seven countries; it even tripled in the United States and France, and increased six times in Japan. The data in Table 3.1 show, moreover, that the rate of growth of these services has not yet slowed down very much. In terms of percentage points, this sector actually grew the most during the 1960s in four countries: the United States, Canada, France, and Japan.

SOCIAL SERVICES SECTOR

One of the main findings of this book, is the fact that social services have been the least affected by economic crises such as the Great Depression or by World War II. Social services increased in all seven countries continuously from decade to decade, without any declines at all. No other industry sector showed a similar expansion of its share of employment. It is particularly noteworthy that most of this increase occurred after 1940, and the rate of growth of social services has not yet slowed down (although that situation might be expected for the United States during the 1970s, since its social services sector already is quite large).

Table 3.4: Employment in Medical Services, Education, and Public Administration: Seven Industrialized Countries, 1970

Country	Medical Services (incl. hospitals)	Education	Public Administration
United States	5.9	8.6	4.6
Canada	5.7	7.3	5.4[b]
England	4.9	5.8	6.0
Germany	3.2	3.0	8.6
France	3.3	4.4	3.3
Italy	a	a	a
Japan	2.0	2.7	3.3[b]

a. No data available.
b. Includes postal service.
Source: See Appendix A.

The three most important social services are medical services (including hospitals), education, and public administration. To the extent that a country such as the United States has a large social service sector as compared to Italy or Japan, it should be expected, of course, that its individual social services are larger. These relationships are upheld in Table 3.4, but the data show some additional interesting findings.

The large size of the social service sector in the United States and Canada is primarily due to their heavy expansion of educational facilities. In 1970, 8.6 percent of all U.S. workers were employed by education alone. This figure is larger by far than that of any other country, and it is truly outstanding considering the fact that in Japan all social services combined employed only slightly more persons (10.2 percent).

The data in Table 3.4 also show that public administration accounts for nearly one-half of the total social services in Germany. In contrast, all other countries except Japan have more persons in education and medical services than has Germany. The low share in education is particularly noteworthy. It largely was the inadequate expansion of educational facilities in postwar Germany that set the stage for the student unrests of the 1960s and early 1970s. The German educational system never quite recovered from its dismantling during the Hitler era.

The structure of secondary and higher education was completely unprepared for the mass influx of students that came about as a result of the postwar baby boom and the general increase in the standard of living.

PERSONAL SERVICES SECTOR

During the fifty-year period, the relative number of personal services workers increased overall in the seven countries, except in the case of England. But most of this increase occurred prior to 1960. During the 1960s, this sector only expanded in Germany and Italy, and these increases were very small.

To fully understand the changes of the personal services sector, one needs to distinguish between domestic service and the remaining personal services. The data in Table 3.5 show that domestic service declined between 1920 and 1970 from one of

Table 3.5: Proportion of Employment in Domestic Service and Other Personal Services: Seven Industrialized Countries, 1920-1970

Industries and Countries	About 1920	About 1930	About 1950	About 1960	About 1970
Domestic Service					
United States	n.a.	6.5	3.2	3.1	1.7
Canada	n.a.	4.2	1.6	1.6	0.7
England	7.5	8.2	2.4	1.6	1.0
Germany	4.4	4.0	3.2	1.5	0.5
France	3.7	3.8	3.1	3.0	2.7
Italy	2.4	3.2	2.2	2.2	a
Japan	2.5	2.7	0.8	0.7	0.3
Other Personal Services					
United States	n.a.	4.7	8.9	8.2	8.3
Canada	n.a	6.1	6.2	8.0	7.8
England	5.4	6.3	8.9	7.4	8.0
Germany	3.3	3.8	3.6	4.9	6.0
France	1.9	3.4	4.3	4.4	5.2
Italy	2.2	2.4	2.5	3.7	a
Japan	2.2	4.6	4.5	6.9	7.3

a. No data available.
Source: See Appendix A.

Table 3.6: Country Ranking by Industry Sectors: Seven Industrialized Countries, 1920-1970

Sectors	About 1920	About 1930	About 1950	About 1960	About 1970
Extractive					
	Italy	Japan	Japan	Japan	Japan
	Japan	Italy	Italy	Italy	
	France	France	France	France	France
	Canada	Canada	Canada	Canada	Canada
	Germany	Germany	Germany	Germany	Germany
	United States	United States	United States	United States	United States
	England	England	England	England	England
Transformative					
	England	England	Germany	Germany	Germany
	Germany	Germany	England	England	England
	United States	France	France	Italy	
	France	United States	United States	France	France
	Canada	Italy	Canada	United States	Japan
	Italy	Canada	Italy	Canada	United States
	Japan	Japan	Japan	Japan	Canada
Distributive Services					
	England	England	United States	Canada	Canada
	Canada	United States	Canada	United States	Japan
	United States	Canada	England	England	United States
	France	Japan	Germany	Japan	England
	Japan	France	Japan	Germany	Germany
	Germany	Germany	France	France	France
	Italy	Italy	Italy	Italy	
Producer Services					
	Canada	Canada	United States	United States	United States
	United States	United States	Canada	Canada	Canada
	England	England	England	England	England
	Germany	Germany	France	Germany	France
	Japan	France	Germany	France	Germany
	France	Italy	Italy	Japan	Japan
	Italy	Japan	Japan	Italy	

Table 3.6: (Continued)

Sectors	About 1920	About 1930	About 1950	About 1960	About 1970
Social Services					
	England	England	United States	United States	United States
	United States	United States	England	Canada	Canada
	Canada	Canada	Germany	England	England
	Germany	Germany	Canada	Germany	Germany
	France	France	France	France	France
	Japan	Italy	Italy	Italy	Japan
	Italy	Japan	Japan	Japan	
Personal Services					
	England	England	United States	United States	Canada
	United States	United States	England	Canada	England
	Germany	Canada	Canada	England	United States
	Japan	Germany	France	Japan	France
	Canada	Japan	Germany	France	Japan
	France	France	Japan	Germany	Germany
	Italy	Italy	Italy	Italy	

Source: Based on Table 3.1.

the largest individual industries to an insignificant size; only France had more than 2 percent of total employment in domestic service by 1970. The other personal services, however, increased rather substantially during those fifty years. The most important expanding services are automobile repair shops, lodging, eating, and drinking places. The latter in particular have expanded substantially after 1950, reflecting an increase in disposable income and a further shift of production from the household to the market economy.

The foregoing discussion concerned employment changes in the six industry sectors over time to find out whether or not universal trends could be identified. Two trends clearly emerged: (1) the proportion of the labor force in the extractive sector declined in all seven countries, and (2) social and producer services are the most persistently growing industries.

The data showed, moreover, that there was remarkable stability over time in the ranking of the seven countries in terms of their sector shares. For example, the country with the lowest share of employment in 1920 (England) remained in that position by 1970 (see Table 3.6). A rank-order analysis of the seven countries for each of the six industry sectors between 1920 and 1960 yielded the following results (starting with the extractive sector): .964, .714, .750, .929, .893, and .571. (Since the Italian data for 1970 are not available, 1960 was chosen for this analysis.) The high stability in most industry sectors seems to have continued during the 1960s; the two major changes in that period were the rapid expansion of transformative industries and distributive services vis-à-vis the growth of these sectors in the other countries.

The Internal Structure of the Service Sector

The second purpose of this chapter is the analysis of the internal structure of the service sector and its changes over time. By eliminating the goods-producing sectors from the analysis, we can probe the question whether or not there exist differences among countries in the pattern of growth of the various types of services. This question is addressed in Table 3.7.

These data magnify the employment trends of the four service sectors which were partly addressed in the previous section of this chapter. Distributive services remained the dominant sector throughout the 1920-1970 period. But its relative share of tertiary employment declined substantially during the 1960s, with the result that in two countries (England and Germany) social services have replaced distributive services as the largest sector. The trends in the other countries (except Japan) make it clear that social services will soon become the major sector for tertiary employment in industrialized countries.

The data show, moreover, that the growth of personal services did not keep pace with the overall expansion of tertiary employment and consequently declined in proportion. The opposite is true for producer services: they have grown much faster than total tertiary employment and have already sur-

Table 3.7: Distribution of Employment Among Service Sectors:
Seven Industrialized Countries, 1920-1970 (in percentages),
(Total services = 100)

Sectors and Countries	About 1920	About 1930	About 1950	About 1960	About 1970
Distributive Services					
United States	48.7	45.4	43.3	39.0	35.9
Canada	51.8	45.0	48.4	44.2	37.8
England	44.2	44.2	41.9	41.6	34.5
Germany	43.0	42.5	43.0	41.1	36.9
France	53.5	46.3	42.5	41.7	35.5
Italy	46.2	44.5	42.2	43.1	a
Japan	52.3	53.2	51.0	49.7	49.8
Producer Services					
United States	7.3	7.4	9.3	11.8	15.1
Canada	10.0	8.1	8.9	9.8	12.0
England	5.9	6.3	7.0	9.5	10.8
Germany	7.6	9.0	6.8	10.5	11.1
France	5.9	7.3	8.0	8.1	12.6
Italy	7.0	7.9	7.6	6.6	a
Japan	3.3	3.1	5.2	7.8	11.2
Social Services					
United States	22.7	21.3	24.0	29.1	35.0
Canada	20.2	21.8	25.2	28.3	34.6
England	20.4	19.8	26.4	29.8	37.4
Germany	21.7	22.6	31.5	32.3	37.9
France	19.7	21.2	27.7	31.3	33.9
Italy	22.0	22.9	31.5	30.9	a
Japan	20.5	18.8	25.2	22.2	22.4
Personal Services					
United States	21.4	25.9	23.4	20.1	14.0
Canada	18.1	25.2	17.4	17.7	15.6
England	29.5	29.6	24.7	19.0	17.3
Germany	27.8	25.9	18.6	16.0	14.2
France	20.8	25.1	21.8	18.8	18.1
Italy	24.7	24.7	18.7	19.4	a
Japan	23.8	24.9	18.5	20.3	16.7

a. No data available.

Source: See Appendix A.

passed the personal services sector in one country (the United States).

The most important finding in Table 3.7 is the remarkable similarity among the countries in terms of the internal structure of the tertiary sector. In other words, the size of the individual service sectors relative to the size of the total tertiary sector is quite similar for industrialized countries (with the exception of Japan). This situation characterizes the social services sector particularly well. Thus, we can say that the overall differences in the size of tertiary employment (see Table 3.1) are much greater than the differences in the internal structure of that sector. As the economy shifts from goods-producing industries to services, distributive and personal services initially provide the major share of employment opportunities. But in the course of that movement towards services, the tertiary sector under-goes an internal restructuring favoring social and producer services.

The only country for which this general description fits less well is Japan. Throughout the 1920-1970 period, its distributive sector made up one-half of total tertiary employment. In con-trast to other industrialized countries, its social service sector expanded very slowly and did not keep pace with the growth of total tertiary employment. In Japan, the sector that most bene-fitted from the changes in the internal structure of tertiary employment was producer services. The reasons as to why these differences in the structure of tertiary employment exist in Japan are not completely clear. Much of it has to do with the fact that was noted earlier concerning the large size of trade. This service accounts for such a large share of total tertiary employment that it depresses the shares for the other services. With regard to the surprisingly small social services sector, it is possible that its explanation lies in part in Japan's different industrial organization (e.g., Dore, 1974). Given the Japanese emphasis on firm-related social welfare programs, some services such as medical services are in part carried out within enter-prises. As a result, persons rendering this service would be classified in the same industry as the good that is produced by

the firm. Given the available data, there is no way of knowing
the extent of this occurrence, but the small size of social service
employment in Japan should be viewed in relation to the form
of industrial organization that is specific to Japan.

Chapter 4

INDUSTRY STRUCTURE OF EMPLOYMENT:

ECONOMIC AND DEMOGRAPHIC CHARACTERISTICS

This chapter addresses the relationship between the industry allocation of the labor force, and three economic and demographic variables: national income, international trade, and urbanization. Its purpose is to find some explanation for the changes in the industry structure over time and its differences among the advanced industrial countries.

The decision to concentrate on variables that are external to the labor force as well as to enterprises contrasts with other approaches, such as Fuchs's (1968) study of services in the United States. He placed great emphasis on the differential growth of output among industry sectors, and was able to show that these differences largely explain the recent growth of service employment. Output has risen much more slowly in services than in manufacturing industries. Although it is unlikely that this finding would be very different in the other countries of this study, data necessary for such an approach unfortunately are not available. Certainly, output and productivity data do exist for some of the countries for recent years, but it is not possible to have a time series for all seven countries.

Moreover, the concern here with the emergence of services makes a consideration of output and productivity particularly difficult, because such information for this group of industries is incomplete. (One example of this situation is the U.S. Bureau of the Census, which conducts industrial censuses for all economic branches in great detail except for services which only are surveyed selectively.)

The subject of productivity in services has been of some concern (see, for example, the various contributions assembled in Fuchs, 1969). Kuznets remarked that the problem is primarily due to the fact that the product of services is intangible (1966:143-144):

> For this reason, and despite the magnitude of the services sector, the measurement of its output is most subject to error, and data and knowledge are far too scanty to permit adequate analysis. It may seem ironic that we know less about this sector which includes groups engaged in the production and spread of basic and applied knowledge, as well as those concerned with political and social decisions, than about the other sectors; but it is not surprising, for activities that are not within the repetitive patterns of large-scale operations are for that reason not readily subject to measurement or analysis.

The measurement problem becomes even more difficult in an historical analysis, owing to changes in the price factor over time. Combined with currency differences, the subject of productivity and output becomes extremely difficult to handle in a precise and systematical manner cross-nationally.

Other factors do not fare much better. In his study of *International Differences in Industrial Structure,* Bain (1968) concentrated on manufacturing organization, and he concluded:

> So far as industrial organization is considered, attention generally centers on the manufacturing sectors of national economies; there is little indeed available on the distributive or the service trades, on utilities, on contracting, or on other non-financial sectors except agriculture (1968:4).

As a result, Bain's study is also restricted to the manufacturing sector of eight countries. To that extent, this analysis should be seen as a preliminary attempt to link a number of variables to labor force changes for the entire industry structure of the economy.

It is realized, of course, that besides the three selected variables many other factors influence the economic structure of a country and its labor force distribution. Some of these factors include capital formation, economic policies, employment legislation, or unionization.

Consider employment legislation, for example. There are tremendous difficulties in covering all of its aspects for the seven countries over the time span of four decades. And even if it is assumed that such information could be obtained, how could it ever be made comparable? At least it can be claimed that comparability is feasible with all of the variables selected to be examined in this study.

The most important casualty of this insistence on comparable data is technology, which in many ways can be regarded as the most powerful variable related to the sectoral transformation of the labor force. Not only do technological changes directly result in changes in the distribution of employment, but technology also affects other variables that are related to the labor force structure. This central role of technology has been widely acknowledged (e.g. Harvard University, 1969; Kindleberger, 1969), although little empirical support for this contention has been demonstrated. It must be emphasized, however, that technology is not to be equated with automation or labor-saving innovations. As was pointed out by Blum (1968), technology can also provide new employment opportunities. This aspect has been elaborated by Landes (1969), whose analysis of technological changes since 1750 in Western Europe revealed the innovative aspects of technology in the Industrial Revolution. At that time it was the introduction of machinery in manufacturing production that provided new sources for work (1969:41). Today, the invention of the computer in the late 1940s has created many new jobs such as operatives, programmers, or system analysts rather than replacing people (as was widely feared). And Mansfield (1968:33-108), for example, found that among firms in the manufacturing sector a positive relationship exists between the number of inventions in a particular establishment and the subsequent size of its manpower.

Because of these two dimensions of technology, mechanization and innovation, no general statement about the nature of the relationship between technology and employment changes can be made. Where mechanization dominates, a deflating effect on employment can be anticipated, while an emphasis on the innovative dimension should result in an increase of the labor force.

This discussion of technology demonstrates that many factors are important in the context of the labor force transformation, although they are not specifically examined in this study. The analysis of the selected variables, therefore, can be meaningful only if they are seen within the larger framework of the prevailing economic and social conditions in a given country, and an attempt will be made to cover some of these variables as extensively as possible.

The main reason for the selection of the three variables, then, was the fact that comparable statistics can be obtained for all countries. Moreover, in reviewing the literature about economic development and its impact on the labor force, it was found that most of these variables had been examined on an isolated basis usually involving only one country. In contrast, this study will investigate the relationships between these variables and the labor force on a comparative level over time.

The first variable, per capita income, was chosen as an indicator of industrial growth in order to make the present analysis comparable to previous studies of the labor force transformation, which focused primarily on per capita income or gross national product (for example, see Clark, 1940; Kuznets, 1965). It will be remembered that Clark (1940) had hypothesized a positive association between per capita income and the proportion of the labor force engaged in service activities. While this hypothesis is not totally rejected here, it is not believed that the hypothesis is very useful because of the heterogeneity of the category "services." This category includes many different economic activities that range from communication to domestic service. From Clark's hypothesis we do not know whether to expect an increase in all services with a rise of per capita income or an increase in only certain kinds of services. This analysis, therefore, will provide an examination of the relationship between economic growth and different kinds of services. Since it is expected that the relationship of per capita income and the changes in various types of services is much more complex than would be the case if services were left at the aggregate level, other variables besides per capita income will be of greater importance than most economic analyses seem to suggest.

The second variable, external trade, is important in regard to the industry structure of a country for several reasons. Generally, there is an interdependence between the consumption potential of an economy and the volume of production, i.e., in a closed system no more goods will be produced than can be consumed. Two countries of similar size, for example, that are also comparable in terms of certain socio-economic characteristics such as per capita income, degree of urbanization, and technology, should be expected to feature a very similar distribution of their labor forces among industries. This function of supply and internal demand, however, is mediated by external trade. Because of close relations of each national economy with the international market and its resulting international division of labor, the closed-system model is not appropriate for the analysis of national labor force trends. Thus, if one of the countries in the previous example is able to export a large part of its manufacturing production to other countries, it can be expected that the employment share of manufacturing in that country will exceed that of a country not exporting on a large scale. This example shows that the degree to which external trade has an impact on the industry structure of employment depends not on the volume of trade per se but rather on its proportion of total production, which can be measured in terms of GNP. If the United States and Germany, for example, had the same volume of exports, the impact would be much larger on the German economy because, proportionately, exports would be much larger in Germany than in the United States. It is therefore to be expected that trade is more important in smaller countries than in larger ones. A distinction must be drawn, however, between exports and imports. It can be assumed that the majority of imports and exports originate in goods-producing industries (mainly agriculture, mining, and manufacturing). Therefore, a large net export sector (i.e., exports minus imports) should be positively associated with the proportion of employment in trade industries, because the imported goods have to be distributed to the final consumer. Finally, these relationships are likely to be affected by the kinds of goods that are being exchanged. Imports of capital goods, for example, require much less manpower for their internal distribution than is the case with consumption goods, because no retail transactions are necessary for the former.

The third variable, population redistribution, is believed to be the most important demographic variable related to employment changes in the selected countries. Given the time period 1920 to 1970, population redistribution refers primarily to urbanization because international migration from Europe to North America was much diminished by the 1920s. Urbanization affects the industrial structure of the labor force in several ways. First, an industrial society, and even more so a service society, is closely associated with a primarily urban population. While many services such as medical service or retail trade can be performed in a rural setting (although on a smaller scale), other services are almost exclusively urban, e.g., subway transportation, higher education, or stock brokers. But in addition, the nature of the urban structure itself is of importance. In a study on "Service Industries and the Urban Hierarchy," Duncan (1959) demonstrated that a certain city size is required for the presence of particular service industries; news syndicates, for example, require a "critical city size" of 250-500,000 persons (1959:115). Or consider the example of a country where 40 percent of the urban population lives in one big city. This would probably mean that the transportation and communication network is less developed than in a country where the largest city accounts for only 10 percent of the urban population, and the remaining 90 percent is distributed among a number of smaller cities. The urban structure of France, for example, is characterized by high primacy (i.e., Paris is over seven times as large as the next largest city, Lyon). It has been noted by Hansen (1968) that this high primacy, with its political and economic concentration in Paris, has resulted in an inadequate and inefficient transportation and communication network. In some cases it is faster to go from one French city to another via Paris, although it means a journey twice the physical distance between these cities. According to Hansen's interpretation, this centralized transportation system contributed a great deal to the relatively slow growth of French industrialization. In such a case, a relatively high proportion of the total labor force in transportation activities in relation to the employment share of manufacturing is expected. On the other hand, primacy has been associated with a large employment share in services (Browning, 1972; Lamberg, 1965), and although these sources refer to Latin America, a similar relationship is anticipated for the countries studied here.

Although it would have been preferable to discuss the relationship between the three variables (national income, international trade, and urbanization) for the same time period chosen for the analysis of the sectoral transformation of the labor force in the seven countries, it is extremely difficult to obtain reliable comparative data for either national income, gross national product, or international trade statistics for the 1920-1950 period. This era was characterized by two important events with wide-ranging economic implications: the World Depression of 1929-1932 and the outbreak of World War II in 1939. The national economies were so affected by these events that national income data, as well as trade statistics do not accurately characterize the economic organization of these countries. It might be argued that this situation would be similarly reflected in the labor force distribution by industries and therefore, such a comparison should be made. It was indeed observed in Chapter 4 that the proportion employed in the transformative sector declined in all countries during the 1920s. Yet that decline in no way measures up to the changes in trade statistics, as Bagwell and Mingay (1970:270) clearly showed: "Between 1929 and 1932 the value of world trade declined by nearly two-thirds and its volume by one-third." Similarly, national income data for 1940 can hardly be compared cross-nationally because the international market and its currency exchange system, for all practical purposes, were suspended for the duration of World War II. It is on the basis of these tremendous methodological difficulties that the decision was made to analyze only the 1950-1970 period in terms of the economic variables.

NATIONAL INCOME

Most studies of the growth of services emphasized per capita income as its main determinant, beginning with Colin Clark's (1940) observation that real income per capita is always associated with a high level of tertiary employment. Clark's findings have largely been supported by subsequent studies that include Kuznets (1957; 1971), Fuchs (1968), and Graf (1968). As was pointed out before, the postulation of the relationship between the level of per capita income and the growth of services has been widely criticized on the grounds that the category of services includes too many hetergeneous industries (see Chapters 1 and 2 for a detailed discussion of these arguments). But none of these critics questioned the validity of that relationship within a given country. It is generally agreed that in the course of economic development, national income and the share of employment in services increase concomitantly. Although it is impossible to obtain comparable cross-national income statistics for the 1920-1940 period, the available data for individual countries show that national income during this time increased in all seven countries. Since it was demonstrated in Chapter 3 that the proportion of services workers increased in all seven countries as well, Clark's hypothesis is valid within the experience of these industrialized countries.

Two important questions remain. First, does the relationship between per capita income and the tertiary employment proportion exist among countries? And second, which types of services are associated with the growth of national income?

Turning our attention to the first issue, the cross-national relationship has been almost completely neglected. Among the few exceptions is a study by Metha (1961) which compares the structure of the urban labor force in Burma and the United States. Despite its restriction to the urban labor force, one finding of the study nevertheless is interesting in the present context. Metha showed that in 1953 the proportion of the Burmese labor force in tertiary industries was slightly larger than that of the United States in 1950. Since the per capita national income of the United States is much larger than that of Burma, Metha's findings do not support the hypothesis as formulated by Clark. Other countries showing a similarly high tertiary employment proportion at a relatively low level of per capita income include Argentina, Uruguay, and Panama. These countries around 1953 had 40-50 percent of their labor force employed by tertiary industries, although their national income per capita was only $250-500 (Lambert, 1965). In comparison, France in 1950 had a per capita income of $1,009, yet its tertiary share of total employment was lower than that of the three Latin American countries. These examples suggest that Clark's hypothesis does not hold for a number of countries with differences in per capita income as great as those existing between industrialized and developing countries.

In order to further examine the relationship for the countries of this study, data for gross national product, national income, and per capita income for the 1950-1970 period are presented in Table 4.1. It is not surprising to find that per capita income increased rather substantially in all seven countries between 1950 and 1970, for this was a period of extraordinary economic growth. Those countries with the lowest per capita income in 1950 experienced the most rapid increase, and the growth is particularly impressive for Japan and Germany. Most of this economic expansion occurred during the 1960s, at the end of which Germany had come into second place in terms of per capita national income, and Japan surpassed Italy and Great Britain for fifth place. The smallest rate of economic growth during the 1960s was registered by Great Britain. This slow expansion, in part, resulted from the decline of the pound sterling vis-à-vis the other western currencies, and in part reflects Britain's increasing difficulties keeping its position in the international market in the aftermath of the dismanteling of the British Empire. Both conditions have come to full light in Britain's economic difficulties of the mid-1970s; as a result, Britain's current per capita income is comparable to that of Italy rather than to the per capita income of the other Western European countries.

The data in Table 4.1 are used to test the following hypothesis: among countries, the higher the level of per capita income, the higher the proportion of tertiary employment. As can be seen in Table 4.2, the data support this hypothesis. For both 1950 and 1960, there is a high rank-order correlation between the two variables (Spearman's rank-order coefficients being .893 and .929, respectively), and the correlation still is moderately high in 1970 (.714). These results, therefore, suggest that Clark's hypothesis is valid among industrialized countries.

The most important analysis, however, concerns the relationship between per capita income and the different types of services. Again, Metha's data for Burma and the United States show that, although the tertiary proportions of the total labor force in these countries are very similar, the United States had a much larger share of employment in business services and professional and related services, whereas Burma had a larger share in retail trade. Similarly, Argentina in 1950 had a larger tertiary sector than France, yet its share of employment in community welfare services was much smaller (Cepal, 1956:38).

This leads us to the second hypothesis: Among countries, the higher the level of per capita income, the larger the proportion of the labor force in producer and social services. Again, this hypothesis is supported by the data in Table 4.3, although the

Table 4.1: National Income, Gross National Product, and Per Capita Income: Seven Countries, 1950-1970

Country	1950			1960			1970			1970 Per Capita Income / 1950 Per Capita Income
	National Income Billion U.S. Dollars	Gross National Product Billion U.S. Dollars	Per Capita Income	National Income Billion U.S. Dollar	Gross National Product Billion U.S. Dollar	Per Capita Income	National Income Billion U.S. Dollars	Gross National Product Billion U.S. Dollars	Per Capita Income	
United States	241.9	284.6	1,602	414.5	502.6	2,296	798.6	976.4	3,899	2.434
Canada	14.1	17.9	1,029	27.3	35.9	1,535	63.1	83.6	2,948	2.869
England	29.9	37.2	594	57.4	71.1	1,098	92.6	120.4	1,662	2.798
Germany	17.7	23.1	370	51.1	65.7	924	183.8	207.3	3,106	8.395
France	21.5	28.1	516	45.9	60.0	1,009	114.3	148.5	2,251	4.362
Italy	11.0	13.9	236	25.1	31.9	512	75.7	93.4	1,411	5.979
Japan	9.4	11.0	113	31.9	38.8	341	172.5	198.5	1,669	14.770

Sources: 1950 - International Monetary Fund, *International Financial Statistics* 13 (January, 1960).
1960 - International Monetary Fund, *International Financial Statistics* 17 (January, 1964).
1970 - International Monetary Fund, *International Financial Statistics* 25 (December, 1972).

Note: The author takes responsibility for the uniform conversion to U.S. dollars and for the computation of the per capita income data.

Table 4.2: National Income, Per Capita, and Employment Proportions of Tertiary Industries: Seven Countries, 1950 and 1960

Country	1950				1960				1970			
	Per Capita National Income	Rank	Percentage Employment in Tertiary Industries	Rank	Per Capita National Income	Rank	Percentage Employment in Tertiary Industries	Rank	Per Capita National Income	Rank	Percentage Employment in Tertiary Industries	Rank
United States	1,602	(1)	51.7	(1)	2,296	(1)	56.1	(1)	3,899	(1)	61.3	(1)
Canada	1,029	(2)	44.7	(3)	1,535	(2)	54.1	(2)	2,948	(3)	60.9	(2)
England	594	(3)	45.7	(2)	1,098	(3)	47.4	(3)	1,662	(6)	52.0	(3)
Germany	370	(5)	36.6	(4)	924	(5)	39.7	(4)	3,106	(2)	45.9	(4)
France	516	(4)	32.9	(5)	1,009	(4)	39.3	(5)	2,251	(4)	43.7	(5)
Italy	236	(6)	25.1	(7)	512	(6)	30.2	(7)	1,411	(7)	37.5	(7)
Japan	113	(7)	28.7	(6)	341	(7)	37.4	(6)	1,669	(5)	41.2	(6)

Sources: Employment: Appendix A and Sorrentino (1971)
Income: Table 4.1

Table 4.3 Rank-Order Correlation Coefficients of Per Capita Income and
Employment Proportions of Service Sectors: Seven Industrialized
Countries, 1950-1970

	Correlation Coefficients		
Sectors	*1950*	*1960*	*1970*
Distributive services	.929	.714	.286
Producer services	1.000	.929	.357
Social services	.821	.964	.543
Personal services	.929	.786	−.143

Note: Italy had to be dropped from the 1970 analysis because of missing data.
Source: See Table 4.2.

relationship has become markedly weaker during the 1960s.
These data also show that during the 1950-1960 period per
capita income was positively associated with the size of all
service sectors. By 1970, however, a weak negative association
emerged between per capita income and the share of employment in personal services. This finding is consistent with the
observation made earlier that personal services decreased during
the 1950-1970 period in those countries that had a high per
capita income (with the exception of Canada). It is concluded
from this analysis that in advanced industrialized countries after
World War II, the level of per capita income is primarily associated with an increase in the proportion employed in social and
producer services.

INTERNATIONAL TRADE

Throughout the discussion of the conditions of economic
development in the seven countries (see Chapter 2), the importance of international trade has been noted. Although this is not
the place to discuss the role of international trade in the theory
of economic development, it is clearly one of the most important features of any economy. Many reasons exist as to why the
volume of trade differs among countries. As Lewis (1955:340)
put it: "The extent to which a country participates in international trade depends partly upon its resources, partly upon the

barriers it places in the way of trade, and partly upon its stage
of economic development." This latter point was elaborated
upon by Kuznets (1966:300-321), who noted that international
trade as a proportion of gross national product (GNP) increased
over time in most of the early industrialized countries until
about World Wai I and subsequently declined. On the other
hand, a comparison of 15 developed countries around
1957-1959 showed that a positive relationship exists between
gross national product and international trade as a proportion
of GNP. Countries with a high GNP were more likely to have a
higher ratio of trade to GNP than countries with lower GNPs.
Although Kuznets did not comment on these differences, they
seem to suggest again that the nature of association between
two variables can vary, depending upon whether it is being
examined cross-nationally or historically within one country.

Among recent treatments of the role of international trade is
Kindleberger's (1962) book *Foreign Trade and the National
Economy,* in which he analyzed the interrelations between
foreign trade and economic growth. His emphasis on a comparative perspective led to the observation that the structure of
foreign trade differs substantially among industries. Around
1955-1958, finished manufacturers, for example, accounted for
only 37 percent of total Canadian exports whereas in Germany
they accounted for 77 percent (Kindleberger, 1962:43 and 80).
This finding is very important, for it points out that the export
dependency of industries varies greatly from one country to
another. In general, it can be assumed that the percent employed in a particular industry is larger in a country where a
large share of its products is being exported, compared with a
country where the output of that industry has the domestic
market as its primary destination. This expectation is based on
the assumption that a certain equilibrium exists between production and consumption in a country; this equilibrium can be
mediated by international trade which brings about an increase
or decrease in national production, depending upon whether
imports or exports prevail. However, three qualifications need

to be made. First, the relationship between exports and employment should be stronger for labor-intensive industries than for industries with a high capital-output ratio because the latter can meet additional demand through the infusion of additional capital rather than employment. Second, the production-consumption ratio varies with the level of per capita income; as per capita income increases, there are changes in the consumption potential for certain goods, depending on their income elasticity. These differences should not be of a large magnitude in the countries that are under consideration here because they all belong to the group of highly industrialized nations. Finally, even when a large proportion of the output in a specific industry is export-bound, this does not necessarily lead to increased employment in that industry if large amounts of similar products are being *imported.* Although such a situation may not often occur within an individual industry, it is more frequent on the level of sectors such as manufacturing which combines a wide range of goods. Thus, the export-employment relationship must be controlled for imports. This is being done by subtracting the value of imports of manufactured goods from the value of exports of manufactured goods resulting in net exports.

This brief discussion leads to the question as to whether or not international trade can be empirically linked to the industry structure of the labor force. Since the major part of international trade results from an exchange of goods, whereas services and gold exchanges play only a minor role, international trade is most likely to be related to goods-producing industries of the extractive and transformative sectors. Of particular interest here is the relationship between trade and manufacturing industries, and data have been obtained for total exports, exports of manufactured goods, and net exports of manufactured goods for the 1950-1970 period (see Table 4.4).

These data clearly show that the value of trade in countries is greatly influenced by population size and the magnitude of the national economy. The United States, for example, has a larger labor force than the total population in each of the other countries (except Japan), and therefore, it should be expected

Table 4.4: Values of Export in Seven Countries: 1950-1970 (in billion U.S. dollars)

Country	1950			1960			1970		
	Total Exports	Exports of Manufactured Goods	Net Exports of Manufactured Goods	Total Exports	Exports of Manufactured Goods	Net Exports of Manufactured Goods	Total Exports	Exports of Manufactured Goods	Net Exports of Manufactured Goods
United States	14,868	8,606	5,486	20,300	13,001	6,679	42,590	30,071	3,309
Canada	3,963	1,648	−773	5,395	2,442	−1,403	16,185	9,959	−765
England	7,212	6,132	4,010	9,901	8,406	4,347	19,351	16,975	5,529
Germany	3,461	2,789	2,167	11,414	10,134	5,661	34,189	30,765	12,958
France	3,036	1,985	1,518	6,863	5,067	2,773	17,924	13,964	1,696
Italy	1,488	882	119	3,649	2,701	828	13,210	11,258	3,422
Japan	1,348	1,185	1,033	4,040	3,602	2,618	19,319	18,117	12,392

Source: United Nations, *Yearbook of International Trade Statistics*, 1953, 1960, and 1972.

to engage in more trade activities. However, these data also show that there is a very substantial variation among countries in terms of net exports of manufactured goods. Throughout the 1950-1970 period, Canada imported more manufactured goods than it exported. Japan and Germany, in contrast, are characterized by very large export surpluses, confirming their roles as the major exporting countries.

In order to control for the effect of different population size on the size of international trade, the per capita value of net exports has been computed (see Table 4.5). These data now make it possible to examine the relationship between exports and employment, and the following hypothesis is tested: Among countries, the higher the per capita value of net exports, the larger the share of the labor force in manufacturing industries.

A rank-order analysis of these two variables yields the following correlation coefficients for 1950-1970 (Spearman's r): .848, .857, .786, respectively. Although the strength of the correlation in 1970 is somewhat weaker, these results are consistent with the hypothesis.

The data in Table 4.5 show that the position of a country in the international system of trade is a good indicator of the size of its manufacturing industries. The large surplus of German and British exports of manufactured goods over imports of these products explains the high concentration of their labor force in manufacturing activities. The leading contributors to this trade surplus of manufactured goods in Germany are chemical industries and, most of all, machinery and transportation equipment industries. This situation is clearly reflected in the strong export orientation of German automobile workers; in the case of Volkswagen, up to one-half of its production is export-bound.

Truly astonishing is the upsurge of net exports in Japan during the 1960s, again confirming Lockwood's (1958) earlier observation that the major expansion of Japan's international trade only came after 1963. This expansion even surpassed the remarkable growth of employment in manufacturing industries,

Table 4.5: Net Exports Per Capita (in 1,000 U.S. Dollars) and Share of Total Employment in Manufacturing: Seven Industrialized Countries, 1950-1970

	1950				1960				1970			
	Per Capita Net Exports	Rank	Percentage Employment in Manufacturing	Rank	Per Capita Net Exports	Rank	Percentage Employment in Manufacturing	Rank	Per Capita Net Exports	Rank	Percentage Employment in Manufacturing	Rank
United States	36.2	(4)	26.3	(4)	37.0	(4)	28.9	(3)	16.2	(6)	25.9	(6)
Canada	−56.2	(7)	25.6	(5)	−78.3	(7)	23.1	(6)	−35.7	(7)	22.0	(7)
England	79.2	(1)	37.2	(1.5)	82.7	(2)	37.4	(2)	99.2	(3)	35.1	(2)
Germany	42.7	(2)	37.2	(1.5)	100.1	(1)	41.6	(1)	219.0	(1)	40.2	(1)
France	36.4	(3)	27.1	(3)	60.7	(3)	28.2	(4)	33.4	(5)	28.2	(4)
Italy	2.5	(6)	23.9	(6)	16.7	(6)	27.4	(5)	63.8	(4)	31.0	(3)
Japan	12.4	(5)	16.1	(7)	28.0	(5)	21.8	(7)	119.8	(2)	26.0	(5)

Sources: Exports: Table 4.3
Employment: Appendix A for all countries except Italy; Sorrentino (1971) for Italy

which is the reason why the relationship among countries between net exports and the size of employment in manufacturing became weaker between 1960 and 1970. (In fact, if Japan were excluded from the analysis, the rank-order correlation between net exports and manufacturing employment during 1950-1970 would increase in strength to .929, .943, and 1.000.) This situation is another illustration for the earlier observation (see Chapter 3) that Japan's industrialization has been achieved without a shift of employment into manufacturing activities as pronounced as in the European countries.

POPULATION REDISTRIBUTION

The relationship between urbanization and economic growth has been widely documented in the literature on economic development and social change (Kuznets, 1955; Gibbs and Martin, 1958; Hoselitz, 1961; Cardoso and Reyna, 1968). By now it is textbook knowledge that a population becomes increasingly urban as its labor force moves from agriculture to other industries. For these reasons, it will suffice to note here that this relationship between urbanization and a decreasing share of employment in extractive industries also exists among the countries of this study (see Table 4.6). The only apparent exception is England, which shows a higher proportion of the population classified as urban in 1930 than in the following decades. However, this is clearly the result of the changing country definition, because the 1920-1930 data refer to England and Wales, whereas they refer to the United Kingdom in the subsequent period. As England and Wales are more urban than the United Kingdom, the changes in Table 4.6 were to be expected. The case of Japan illustrates how closely urbanization and the movement out of agriculture are associated. In contrast to Japan's rapid urbanization during the 1930s (and after 1950), the urban percent declined slightly between 1940 and 1950 from 37.9 to 37.5 percent. It was precisely during this same decade that the proportion employed in the extractive sector increased from 46.3 percent in 1940 to 50.3 percent in 1950.

Although it was shown previously that relationships can

Table 4.6: Urban Population as Proportion of Total Population and Employment Shares of Extractive Industries: Seven Industrialized Countries, 1920-1970

Country	Proportion Urban										Proportion Extractive									
	About 1920	Rank	About 1930	Rank	About 1950	Rank	About 1960	Rank	About 1970	Rank	About 1920	Rank	About 1930	Rank	About 1950	Rank	About 1960	Rank	About 1970	Rank
United States	51.2	(3)	56.2	(3)	64.0	(3)	69.9	(3)	75.2	(4)	28.9	(6)	25.4	(6)	14.4	(6)	8.1	(6)	4.5	(6)
Canada	47.4	(4)	52.5	(4)	61.7	(4)	68.6	(4)	74.7	(5)	36.9	(4)	34.4	(4)	21.6	(4)	14.7	(4)	9.1	(4)
England[1]	79.3	(1)	80.0	(1)	77.5	(1)	78.3	(1)	79.1	(3)	14.2	(7)	11.8	(7)	8.9	(7)	6.6	(7)	4.2	(7)
Germany	64.4	(2)	67.1	(2)	72.5	(2)	77.6	(2)	82.2	(2)	33.5	(5)	31.5	(5)	16.1	(5)	9.0	(5)	5.1	(5)
France	46.3	(5)	50.8	(5)	54.1	(5)	61.3	(6)	67.9	(6)	43.6	(3)	38.3	(3)	31.9	(3)	23.0	(3)	17.0	(3)
Italy	40.0[2]	(6)	44.6	(6)	44.0	(6)	47.8	(7)	41.5	(7)	57.1	(1)	48.1	(2)	42.9	(2)	29.8	(2)	20.5	(1)
Japan	18.1	(7)	24.1	(7)	37.4	(7)	63.5	(5)	83.2	(1)	56.3	(2)	50.9	(1)	50.3	(1)	34.1	(1)	20.0	(2)

Notes:
1. The data for England refer to England and Wales in 1920-30 and to the United Kingdom in 1950-70.
2. Estimate

Sources for Urbanization Data:
United States, 1920-1930: Taeuber and Taeuber, 1971: 53.
Canada, 1920-1930: Stone, 1967:29.
England, 1920-1930: United Nations, 1952: Table 6.
Germany, 1920-1930: Hoffmann, 1965: 178.
France, 1920-1930: Annuaire Statistiques, 1966:23.
Italy, 1930: United Nations, 1952: Table 6.
Japan, 1920-1930: United Nations, 1952: Table 6.
All 1950-1970 data: Davis, 1969: Table C.

differ substantially, depending upon whether they are analyzed historically within countries or cross-nationally at a given point in time, the more important issue here concerns the cross-national analysis. Therefore, the relationship among the seven countries between the proportion urban and the relative size of extractive industries is being analyzed for the 1920-1970 period. The results show a strong negative rank-order correlation between the two variables for the 1920-1969 period and a weak, but negative, correlation for 1970. The respective correlation coefficients (Spearman's r) from 1920 to 1970 are: - .929, - .964, - .764, and - .357. The reason for the lower correlation coefficients in 1960 and 1970, compared to the previous years, is the fact that Japan's urbanization during that period proceeded much faster than the movement of its labor force out of agriculture. If Japan is excluded from the analysis, the strong negative association between urbanization and extractive employment continues among the remaining countries for the 1960-1970 period.

Another way of identifying the differences in the urban structure of a society is to examine the distribution of the population among size classes of cities. In a study of "Urbanization and the Development of Preindustrial Areas," Davis and Golden (1954), for example, found a positive correlation between industrialization (as measured by the proportion of gainfully occupied males in nonagricultural occupations) and the proportion of the population in cities over 100,000 persons. The growth of large cities has a special relevance for the present study, because services are primarily urban activities. In fact, some services require rather large population concentrations, such as specialized hospital facilities or airports (see Duncan, 1959). It is thus expected that there is a positive association among countries between the percent of the population residing in cities over 100,000 persons and the proportions of total employment in the four service sectors. A similar association should exist between this measure of the urban structure and the relative size of the transformative sector. Finally, following

the previously observed negative association between percent
urban and the relative size of extractive employment, a similar
relationship should exist between the existence of large cities
and employment in extractive industries. These relationships are
tested by means of rank-order analysis, and the correlation
coefficients (Spearman's r) are given in Table 4.7.

Corresponding to Davis and Golden's (1954) findings, these
data show that the proportion of the population in cities over
100,00 persons is negatively associated with the proportion of
the share of employment in extractive industries. All nonextractive industry sectors are positively associated with cities over
100,000 population, as was anticipated. Moreover, this association is stronger for the service sectors than for transformative
employment, particularly after 1950.

However, the data do show a substantial decline of the
relationships during the 1960s; only the negative association
between large cities and extractive employment remained strong
by 1970. One could expect that once urbanization reaches the
high level, as it exists in the advanced industrialized countries,
cities with a population of over one million—rather than
100,000—may be more appropriate as an indicator of differences in the urban structure. But the results of that analysis did
not fare much better. The correlation coefficients did increase

Table 4.7: Rank-Order Correlation Coefficients of Population Proportions
Residing in Cities over 100,000 and Employment Shares of Industry
Sectors: Seven Industrialized Countries, 1950-1970

	Correlation Coefficients		
	1950	1960	1970
Extractive	−.857	−.857	−.786
Transformative	.679	.393	.071
Distributive services	.714	.571	.200[*]
Producer services	.464	.679	.243[*]
Social services	.786	.617	.314[*]
Personal services	.643	.464	.148[*]

[*]Owing to missing data, Italy was excluded from the analysis.
Source: Urbanization data are computed from Davis, 1969: Table C.

for all sectors (except distributive services), but the largest coefficient for the nonextractive industries was only .429 (for social services). It can be concluded from these findings that the historical relationship between size classes of cities and the relative shares of employment in nonextractive industry sectors seem to disappear. Apparently, once the proportion of the population in large cities is as high as in the case of industrialized countries, it bears little relationship to the sectoral allocation of employment.

Chapter 5

FROM AGRICULTURE TO SERVICES:

A DISTINCTIVE PATH?

The last two chapters examined the sectoral transformation of the labor force in the major industrialized countries and its relationship to national income, international trade, and urbanization. In this chapter, I wish to examine the pattern of this transformation in those countries. It will become clear in the discussion that this analysis has important consequences for the evaluation of the employment structure in developing countries. In a final section, I shall discuss the direction of that transformation, and particularly the outlook for a further expansion of services, during the remainder of the twentieth century.

Three Patterns of the Sectoral Transformation

A comparison of the sectoral transformation of the labor force in the seven countries reveals that the three geographic areas—North America, Western Europe, and Japan—each represent a distinct pattern of that transformation.

WESTERN EUROPE

In the four European countries, the decline of agriculture resulted primarily in the growth of transformative industries.

Although producer and social services expanded as well during the four decades, transformative industries nevertheless remained the dominating sector of the labor force. This pattern can be illustrated in several ways. For one, England and Germany in 1920 already had a larger proportion of their respective labor force in the transformative sector than the United States did in 1960 (the year its transformative sector reached the peak). And France, in 1930, surpassed the United States in terms of proportionate transformative employment, notwithstanding the fact that in 1930 its extractive employment share was much larger than that of the United States. Even Italy, whose extractive sector was about twice as large as that of the United States throughout the five decades, had only a slightly smaller transformative sector than the United States through 1950, and it then pulled far ahead in the following decades. Second, all four European countries since 1920 had at least as much and often more employment in transformative industries than in all services sectors combined (see Table 5.1). The only exception is England where the transformative sector had slightly less employment than the four services sectors together. Third, the most important support for this sectoral transformation pattern comes from the fact that it is followed by the countries regardless of their phase of economic development. While England and Germany were already fully industrialized in 1920, the main shift from agricultural to nonextractive employment in Italy occurred during the 1950s. But as the data in Table 3.1 show, the proportion of Italy's employment in the transformative sector is rapidly expanding, and the typical pattern that was followed by the other three countries is already established in Italy. Time seems to play only a minor role as far as the sectoral transformation of the labor force in Europe is concerned.

NORTH AMERICA

The second pattern of the sectoral transformation of the labor force is followed by Canada and the United States. In contrast to the European nations, these two countries already

Table 5.1: Percentage Distribution of Employment by Industry Sectors: Seven Industrialized Countries, 1920-1970

Countries and Year	Extractive	Transformative	Services	Total
United States				
1920	28.9	32.9	38.2	100.0
1930	25.4	31.5	43.1	100.0
1950	14.4	33.9	51.7	100.0
1960	8.1	35.9	56.1	100.1
1970	4.5	33.9	61.6	100.0
Canada				
1921	36.9	26.1	37.0	100.0
1931	34.4	24.7	40.9	100.0
1951	21.6	33.7	44.7	100.0
1961	14.7	31.2	54.1	100.0
1971	9.1	30.0	60.9	100.0
England				
1921	14.2	42.2	43.6	100.0
1931	11.8	39.3	48.9	100.0
1951	8.9	45.4	45.7	100.0
1961	6.6	46.0	47.4	100.0
1971	4.2	43.8	51.9	99.9
Germany				
1925	33.5	38.9	27.6	100.0
1933	31.5	38.3	30.2	100.0
1950	16.1	47.3	36.6	100.0
1961	9.0	51.3	39.7	100.0
1970	5.1	49.0	45.9	100.0
France				
1921	43.6	29.7	26.7	100.0
1931	38.3	32.8	28.9	100.0
1954	31.9	35.2	32.9	100.0
1962	23.0	37.7	39.3	100.0
1968	17.0	39.3	43.7	100.0
Italy				
1921	57.1	24.2	18.7	100.0
1931	48.1	29.2	22.7	100.0
1951	42.9	32.0	25.1	100.0
1961	29.8	40.0	30.2	100.0
1970	20.1	42.4	37.5	100.0
Japan				
1920	56.3	19.7	24.0	100.0
1930	50.9	19.8	29.3	100.0
1950	50.3	21.0	28.7	100.0
1960	34.1	28.5	37.4	100.0
1970	20.0	34.3	45.6	99.9

Source: See Appendix A

had more employment in services than in the transformative sector in 1920, and that gap widened continuously through 1970. This trend has recently been reinforced by the relative decline of the transformative sector that began in Canada in 1950 and in the United States ten years later. All present signs point against a reversal in that trend, and it can safely be assumed that the transformative sector has reached its peak in both countries. It is of interest, again, that both countries followed a very similar path of the sectoral transformation, despite the fact that Canada continued to have a larger representation in extractive industries than the United States.

JAPAN

The third pattern of the sectoral transformation of the labor force is represented by Japan. Although Japan is comparable to Italy in terms of extractive employment, it resembles the North American countries in the fact that the proportion employed in the four service sectors combined has always been larger than that in the transformative industries. In contrast to Canada or the United States where services and transformative industries expanded simultaneously (with services ultimately pulling ahead), the decline of agriculture in Japan directly led to a predominance of services. It was only during the 1960s that Japan's transformative sector reached one-third of total employment.

The Japanese pattern is very surprising, indeed. During the past twenty-five years, Japan has become one of the world's leading industrial nations, yet its proportion of the labor force in transformative industries is smaller than that of France or Italy.

One explanation for Japan's ability to achieve its present volume of production with a relatively small proportion of the labor force in the transformative sector is technology. Cole (1973:434) has called attention to the fact that Japanese workers and trade unions only offer few objections to technological innovations in factories because the Japanese system of permanent employment guarantees the worker his job. "Permanent employment, or the lifetime employment system as it is sometimes called, refers to the practice by which male employees, especially those in large firms are hired on graduation from middle school, high school or college, receive in-company training and remain employees in the same company until retirement at fifty-five. So conscious are the Japanese of the different status of job changers that they commonly use a special term, *chúto saiyosha,* to designate such individuals" (Cole, 1973:429). Other students of the Japanese employment structure have arrived at the same conclusion (for example, see Nakane, 1972:104-120). Given Japan's disposition to use the most modern existing technology, it does not seem very likely that its transformative sector will expand much beyond one-third of the labor force, whereas the continuing decline of agricultural employment should result in a steady growth of services.

Implications for Contemporary Industrialization

It is clear now that only the European countries are following the Fisher-Clark thesis of employment shifts from primary to secondary and, subsequently, to tertiary industries. Even the United States and Canada do not fit their model, and Japan's experience has been completely different.

The Japanese case has some important implications for the situation of industrializing nations. It demonstrates that the time of industrialization is a crucial factor that must be taken into consideration. To use Veblen's notion of the "advantage of backwardness": what took England one hundred years was accomplished by Germany in fifty and it required only twenty years in Japan. The key variable here is technology and its transferability. Factors in industrializing countries reflect the technological know-how of industrialized countries, for they supply the capital equipment. The new automobile industries in Brazil, for example, use more modern production techniques than many of their counterparts in Europe or the United States.

Thus, transformative industries in developing countries require much less employment than industrialized countries at comparable moments of economic growth, for their output per worker is much higher. As a result, the decline of agriculture is not being absorbed by the transformative sector but leads instead to the growth of employment in services. In that sense, it is not completely the insufficient development of the transformative sector, but also its higher level of technology that results in the direct shift in the industry structure from agriculture to services in industrializing countries.

It is equally clear, of course, that the existing international division of labor greatly disfavors the industrializing countries, and this situation has been widely discussed in the dependency literature for Latin America (Cardoso, 1970; Jaguaribe et al., 1970; Cockcroft et al., 1972). As long as the international system of trade virtually guarantees the major industrialized countries an export market for their manufactured goods with their high degree of value added, it will be very difficult for the developing countries to brake the barrier of sustained economic growth. To analyze the position of developing countries in the international system of trade, indicators other than employment in manufacturing are preferable, because the Japanese example illustrates that a small transformative sector can conceal a substantial economic force.

A second reason for the faster development of service industries in Japan (and in developing countries of today) is its more rapid pace of urbanization. An urban society requires more services than a rural society, because cities depend on electricity, sanitation services, transportation, trade, and the like. In that sense, developing countries need to have more employment in services than what might be expected from the experience of industrial countries.

Another difference between the industrial countries and the developing nations concerns the scope of social legislation. Many developing countries of today have more extensive social programs than their industrial counterparts had when they industrialized. After all, Bismarck's social legislation of the

1880s was the first in Europe of its scope, and even at the turn of the century, England was far away from governmental commitment to social welfare.

Finally, what sets the European countries apart from all other nations in their period of industrialization was their ability to "export" people. As agriculture rapidly increased its productivity and began to release scores of workers who were no longer needed in agricultural production, many of them could emigate to the Americas. In the absence of that "safety valve," many of them would probably have been channeled into some type of service activities. Neither Japan, Canada, the United States, nor Latin America had this possibility, and the main problem of developing countries is not the emigration of agricultural workers but the "brain drain" of highly skilled persons to North America and Europe.

In sum, the conditions under which Japan industrialized were quite different from those encountered by the European or North American countries. This situation in turn required a different pattern of the sectoral transformation in Japan than in the earlier industrialized countries. And for the same reasons it can be expected that developing countries, even more so than Japan, will largely bypass the manufacturing sector in terms of employment from an agricultural to a service society. Thus, it is suggested here that the direct transformation from an agricultural to a service labor force not be viewed a priori in negative terms (as has sometimes been done with respect to Latin America), because it is becoming clear that the traditional model of the sectoral transformation of the labor force, with its sequence from primary to secondary and, then, to tertiary production, is the exception rather than the rule. Moreover, the Japanese case illustrates that the phase during which secondary employment is the dominant sector of the labor force is not a necessary condition for successful and sustained economic development. Rather, much greater emphasis than is done today should be placed on an examination of the mix of services, i.e., the internal structure of the tertiary sector. On the basis of such careful differentiation of the various types of services in a particular country, it would be possible to evaluate which services should become the target of developmental policies. There are many services such as banking, insurance, recreation, or tourism, that can be developed simultaneously with selected manufacturing industries, and the growth of these services would stimulate rather than impair economic development. While a model of service based economic development has not yet been constructed, some interest in such an approach is emerging, as exemplified by Puerto Rico which has been examining its service sector in order to identify those individual services, the growth of which would be beneficial for economic growth and employment.

The Growth of Services: A Look Into the Future

The past fifty years have witnessed a tremendous change in the industry structure of the major industrialized countries. In 1920 most of their economies were strongly oriented toward agriculture, yet by 1970 the extractive sector had become the smallest sector in three of the seven countries. Although all other industry sectors benefited from this decline of extractive activities, producer and social services showed the most rapid gains. Is this sweeping transformation of employment that has characterized the past fifty years likely to continue through the end of this century at a similar pace? The answer must be no. It seems that we have seen the largest part of that transformation in most of the countries, with the exceptions of France, Italy, and Japan which still have a moderately large extractive sector. In the following section it will be attempted to chart the probable development of the six industry sectors for the remainder of the twentieth century.

There can be no doubt that the extractive sector will continue its decline in those countries in which its share of total employment is still moderately high (Japan, Italy, and France). The changes in modern agriculture—among them are increased capital equipment, new types of seeds and fertilizers, and the development of agro-business—all point toward a future reduc-

tion in agricultural employment. The most recent employment
surveys support this expectation: During the early 1970s the
extractive sector continued its rapid decline in Japan, Italy, and
France. However, the case of the United States and Germany
(and presumably England, if mid-1970 data were available for
that country) demonstrate that once this sector is reduced to
about 4-5 percent of total employment, further decreases are
not very likely (see Table 5.2). It must also be remembered in
this context that the beginning of the 1970s brought an end to
most agricultural surpluses that existed in the previous two
decades. As a result of several bad harvests around the world
and a continued high rate of world population growth, demand
for food increased substantially and may in part explain the
slight increase in agricultural employment in the United States
from 1970 to 1974.

It seems that the transformative sector has reached its peak
share of total employment in all countries except Japan. This
sector declined in four of the seven countries during the

Table 5.2: Employment by Industry Sector: Six Industrialized Countries,
1974 (in percentages)

Country	Extractive	Transformative	Services	Total
United States	4.8	32.5	62.8	100.1
percent change from 1970	0.3	− 1.4	1.2	
Canada (1975)	8.0	28.1	63.8	99.9
percent change from 1971	−1.1	− 1.9	2.9	
Germany	5.2	48.9	45.9	100.0
percent change from 1970	0.1	− 0.1	0.0	
France	12.3	37.8	49.7	99.8
percent change from 1968	− 4.7	− 1.5	6.0	
Italy (1975)	15.7[1]	43.9[2]	40.4	100.0
percent change from 1970	− 4.4	1.5	2.9	
Japan	13.3	36.7	50.0	100.0
percent change from 1970	− 6.7	2.4	4.4	

1. Excludes mining.
2. Includes mining.
Source: International Labour Office, *Yearbook of Labor Statistics 1975,* Table 2.

1960-1970 period, and that trend continued during the first half of the 1970s. Even Japan's expansion of employment in transformative industries slowed down in the 1970-1974 period, and it is not expected to ever reach the level of employed that was characteristic of Germany and England in the 1950s and 1960s.

The mid-1970 employment surveys in the six countries unfortunately do not allow a disaggregation of the various service sectors. The data for services as a whole clearly show that this sector is continuing its expansion of employment in the 1970s. As far as distributive services are concerned, all countries had a higher proportion employed in that sector in 1970 than in 1920 (except for England). During that same period, distributive services increased at a slower rate than the nonextractive labor force as a whole, which suggests that they should remain at about the same level or slightly decline in the near future, once the shift out of agriculture comes to a halt. If the European countries should decide, however, to implement the same quality of retail services (in terms of store hours and number of retail locations) that can be found in the United States, their distributive service sector would have to increase considerably. Several reasons speak against such a shift. First, their continued emphasis on transformative industries is likely to provide employment opportunities in industries with greater productivity and higher wage rates compared to retailing. Second, in a country such as Germany, both small shopkeepers and the labor unions form a powerful alliance that is opposed to any extension of store hours, and there are no indications for a change in their stand. Finally, the increased concern about the use of energy and its cost would make it unlikely to extend store hours, and to employ a second work shift because that would substantially raise the energy input per given unit of retail volume.

It has repeatedly been mentioned that producer and social services proved to be the two most rapidly growing industry sectors. Not only did they increase their employment share of the total labor force, they also grew faster than nonextractive employment. Most of this increase occurred after World War II, and it is expected that their expansion will continue in the next decades. In light of the current economic difficulties of the major industrialized countries and their increasing budget deficits, it is likely that the rate of expansion of social services will decline in the coming years, particularly in the United States, Canada, and England where social services already account for one-fifth or more of total employment. The most rapid growth of social services should occur in Japan where it employed only one-tenth of all workers in 1970.

Finally, the heterogeneity of personal services makes it extremely difficult to isolate past changes, not to mention future trends. It can be seen in Table 3.1 that the share of total employment in personal services alternately grows and declines between 1920 and 1960. During the 1960s, however, it remained remarkably stable in all countries except the United States where it declined substantially. It seems that once domestic service has reached a negligible proportion of total employment (around 1-2 percent), as it is already the case in Canada, England, Germany, and Japan, the proportion employed in the total sector will remain fairly stable.

Although it is often assumed that the demand for personal services increases with rising per capita income, the available data do not support that assumption, even when the effect of declining domestic service is taken into consideration. Apparently, the demand for personal services can be met in part through capital inputs instead of labor. Consider the case of laundries. While a certain per capita income is necessary before laundry services can be utilized, the experience of the industrialized countries shows that washing machines at home and coin operated laundromats can meet the demand for laundry services without increasing employment. These appliances have made the task of washing easy enough that it can be performed by the customer himself.

A similar situation exists in food services. From 1920 to 1950 the proportion employed by eating and drinking places increased substantially but since then the rate of growth leveled

off. Greater capital intensity and labor saving forms of organization in food services make it possible to meet higher demand
without a proportionate increase in employment. These trends
form part of the larger shift of capital into the newer personal
services that have been discussed in the recent work by Mandel
(1968; 1972). Even assuming that an increasing part of personal
services which traditionally have been carried out in the household will be performed outside the house, it is not believed that
the personal services sector will grow beyond the present levels.

On the basis of these considerations, an attempt has been
made to project the proportion of the labor force in each
industry sector by the end of this century, and the results are
presented in Table 5.3. To arrive at these data, the past employment trends in the respective countries have been extrapolated
and in addition, possible changes in the variables that were
discussed in Chapter 5 have been taken into account. In each
country group, the first column represents an average of the
proportion of employment in each industry sector in 1970,
whereas the second column indicates an estimation of the
proportion of the total labor force that each industry sector will
account for in the year 2000. These projections must be taken
only as rough approximations, and the actual proportions may
very well differ by some percentage points. It is believed,

Table 5.3: Projection of the Labor Force Distribution by Industry Sectors
in the Year 2000: Seven Industrialized Countries

Industry Sectors	United States Canada		England Germany		France Italy		Japan	
	1970	2000	1970	2000	1970	2000	1970	2000
Extractive	7	- 5	5	- 4	19	- 10	20	- 5
Transformative	32	- 28	47	- 40	41	- 35	34	- 40
Distributive services	23	- 20	17	- 16	15	- 15	23	- 20
Producer services	8	- 12	5	- 10	4	- 10	5	- 10
Social services	21	- 30	18	- 25	15	- 25	10	- 20
Personal services	9	- 6	8	- 5	7	- 5	8	- 5
	100	100	100	100	100	100	100	100

Source: Based on Table 3.1.

however, that the foregoing discussion of the national labor force trends offered enough information to consider these figures adequate approximations.

A comparison of the four country groups shows that there will be very little variation in the share of total employment in the extractive sector by the year 2000. Most of the differences will be accounted for by the transformative industries, and the distributive and social services. England, Germany, and Japan are expected to have around 40 percent of their labor force in the transformative sector, followed by Italy and France with around 35 percent. In the United States and Canada, this proportion could go as low as one-fourth.

For the reasons that were previously discussed, the least change should occur in distributive services, and it is expected that the present differences between the country groups in terms of employment in their sector will remain. By the end of the century most countries are expected to have about ten percent of total employment in producer services, and the United States and Canada are most likely to exceed that percentage; a proportion of 12-15 percent for the United States does not seem unlikely.

Despite the present worldwide economic difficulties and the concern of industrialized countries about an overcommitment to the welfare state, it seems most likely that social services will continue to increase their share of total employment. In part, the existing social legislation in these countries virtually secures a certain level of employment opportunities and there are no signs of a serious reversal of this direction. Even when the Social Democrats in Sweden after forty years in power were replaced by a coalition of Conservative parties, no attempt was made to dismantle the Swedish welfare state. In part, the growth of social services must also be seen in light of the productivity gains in agriculture and manufacturing. Since these goods-producing industries can meet an increasing demand partly through greater capital infusion, they need not expand their employment as much as would be necessary in most services. Finally, many social services respond to increased demand with more employment, but when the demand diminishes, the peak employment levels are maintained, owing to the sheltered job conditions of many social service employees. There exists a tendency among social service agencies to create new demand themselves by budgeting additional positions, because the size of an agency and the amount of its budget often represent a certain degree of power within the larger governmental bureaucracy. All these tendencies affect the level of employment in social services in a positive way. Thus, it is expected that by the end of this century all countries will have at least 20 percent of their labor force in social services. In the European countries, it may be as high as one-fourth, and the United States and Canada might reach 30 percent. The projection for the relative size of social services in these two countries in the year 2000 is particularly difficult because this sector already is very large. Since it was concluded earlier that the extractive sector will no longer be a source of the sectoral transformation, it appears that the size of social services largely hinges on the development of the transformative sector. It seemed until very recently that the transformative sector would continue its proportionate decline that began in Canada in the 1950s and ten years later in the United States. However, with the recent decline of the U.S. dollar, and the even more dramatic loss in value of the Canadian dollar, foreign investments in these two countries have become attractive to many nations, particularly in Europe. The result has been a surge of acquisitions of U.S. firms by European capital, or the construction of completely new production facilities in the U.S., and 1977 marked the first year after World War II that foreign investment in the United States exceeded the investment of U.S. capital abroad. To the extent that this trend continues, the decline of employment in the transformative sector should, at least, slow down, with social services expanding correspondingly less. Thus, the projected proportions for the transformative and social services sectors in the year 2000 should be viewed as the minimal and maximal size, respectively, and it is possible that social services will account for a share of total employment that is closer to 25 percent than to 30 percent.

As difficult as it is to project any employment changes in personal services, it is believed that this sector will account for 5-6 percent of total employment in industrialized countries by the year 2000.

In summary, the discussion in this chapter has shown that the differences among industrialized countries in the industry structure of their labor force are becoming smaller as all countries complete their shift from agricultural to nonextractive employment, but it is not expected that these differences will disappear by the end of this century. A convergence of the industry structures of industrialized countries, therefore, does not seem very likely in the next 25 years, provided that their present economic and demographic characteristics change similarly in the near future. What seems clear is that producer services and particularly social services will be the main beneficiaries of the future employment shifts, although the level of employment in social services will still vary among the countries by the end of the twentieth century. Most important of all, the data clearly showed that the industrialized countries are following quite different patterns in transforming their economies from an agricultural orientation to a service orientation.

Chapter 6

SOME DIMENSIONS OF A SERVICE SOCIETY:

A RESEARCH AGENDA

The preceding analysis of the sectoral transformation of the labor force in the major industrial countries of the capitalist economy revealed that in the past fifty years, service employment grew much faster than the nonagricultural labor force. Today services employ over one-half of all workers in four of the seven countries, and their share exceeds 60 percent in the United States and Canada. It was also shown that there has been an important restructuring of the tertiary sector during that time from distributive and personal services to producer and social services. It is the latter two types of services that have been expanding most rapidly and continuously in all countries. The universal growth of these services is particularly remarkable in view of the persisting differences in the industry structure of these countries and their different patterns of the sectoral transformation.

The most advanced industrial countries have either already developed a service economy or are rapidly moving toward one. If the future employment opportunities are to be provided mostly by the various service industries—and many signs point to that direction—we must come to a better understanding of the environment in which this development takes place, and of the economic and sociological consequences of this shift in the industry structure of employment.

Such a position implies that the characteristics of service industries are sufficently different from those of goods-producing industries that the growth of services represents a qualitatively different development than a shift of employment from one manufacturing industry to another. After the preceding discussion about the importance of distinguishing different types of services, the unqualified dichotomy of goods-producing industries versus service industries is untenable. On the other hand, there are some characteristics which appear to be more applicable to services in general than to goods-producing industries, and although there does not yet exist sufficient information to permit a comprehensive comparison of the nature of these differences (largely because of inadequate statistics about service industries), a first step toward such comparison can be taken.*

Some Characteristics of Service Industries

The central feature of services that distinguishes them from other industries is the absence of a tangible product. This characteristic has several important ramifications for work and its organization. Associated with the nonmaterial product of services is the difficulty to stockpile them. As a result, the production of services is closely linked to their consumption: in many cases, production and consumption of services occur at the same time. This situation creates special problems for the scheduling of production hours and for the organization of work, even in those cases where the demand can somewhat be channeled through office hours and appointments. Perhaps the best example for the variation in demand are eating and drinking places, which experience two peak periods daily that require substantially more employment than the remaining hours of the day.

---

*This topic is currently being pursued by Harley L. Browning and myself in a separate project.

Another characteristic of the intangible nature of services is the lesser standardization of their products. As a result, the assemblyline process of production is less appropriate for services, there is less segmentation of the work tasks, and more case-by-case decisions are required from the workers. (These descriptions of work in services obviously are more applicable to some occupational positions within services than others; the point here is that the degree of task segmentation, on the average, is lower in services than in other industries.)

Yet with respect to many of the features of services, tendencies are clearly apparent to organize service industries in a fashion similar to that in manufacturing industries; this development will become accelerated with the transfer of more private capital into the various service industries. At this point, however, the intangible nature of services is viewed by many as the main reason for the need to adapt the concepts of economic analysis to the emergence of a service economy, as illustrated in the following section.

Economic Implications of the Growth of Services

In his book *The Service Economy,* Fuchs (1968: 194-195) observed that productivity in many services depends to a large degree on the "consumer as a cooperating agent in the production process. In the supermarket and laundromat the customer actually works, and in the doctor's office the quality of the medical history the patient gives may influence significantly the productivity of the doctor."

The growth of services can also influence the relationship of labor and capital. While economic theory "traditionally assumed that capital is a fixed factor and that labor is variable" (Fuchs, 1968:196), this is not true for many service industries. Much capital equipment can be leased today (such as office machinery and computers), whereas employment in the government sector, for example, often cannot be discharged at will. Moreover, given the greater labor intensity in services than in goods-producing industries, the former must rely more on labor-embodied technology which can usually be upgraded only through a replacement of older workers by new employees.

Despite the large amount of capital investments in such services as hospitals and communication, most service industries remain less conducive to the introduction of technological innovations. This will have an important effect of slowing down the rate of growth of a country's economy, and it is no coincidence that the contemporary discussion of the future of growth (in economic or demographic terms) parallels the emergence of a service economy.

Finally, the lesser use of material technology in service industries also means that service establishments, on the average, are smaller than establishments in the transformative sector. Again, this situation has implications for the organization of work and for the way employees perceive their jobs. Smaller establishments can make work more personal but they may not be able to offer the range of fringe benefits that larger establishments can afford.

Whether the shift toward services will mean "an end to the myth of the domination of the large corporation in our society," as Fuchs (1968: 10) speculated, remains to be seen. There exists an important difference between *establishments* and *enterprises* or *firms* (see Pryor's fascinating book, *Property and Industrial Organization in Communist and Capitalist Nations,* (1973) for more information on this subject). Fast-food chains are a good illustration of this: although the size of a McDonald's or Burger King restaurant (establishment) is often very small, it belongs (if it is not franchised) to a large corporation (enterprise), in this case McDonald's and Pillsbury, respectively (see also Levitt, 1976). And even in the case of franchised establishments, there are close connections between the establishment and the franchisor, including quality control, content of the menu, and advertising. Moreover, both Mandel (1968; 1972) and Braverman (1974) have called attention to the increasing shift of corporate capital into a variety of services that traditionally were owner-operated businesses or one-establishment firms. Their basic thesis is that in a service economy many of the traditionally petty bourgeois economic activities will become organized along the capitalist mode of production.

While there are other important economic consequences of the growth of services that could be noted here, they have received more attention than have the sociological implications of the sectoral transformation. Therefore, the remainder of this chapter will point out some of the most essential features.

Sociological Aspects of a Service Economy

The emergence of a service economy has been viewed by many sociologists as one marker for the transition from an industrial to a postindustrial society. But despite the increasing interest in the sociological dimensions of a postindustrial, or service society (Bell, 1976, 1973; Gartner and Riessman, 1974; Touraine, 1971), there exists no consensus as to the definition of such society. There is not even a common term to describe the advanced industrial societies: while the affix "post" is most frequently used, it ranges from "postbourgeois" society to "postwelfare" society (see the subject index in Bell (1973) for further variants). The absence of a proper definition makes it impossible to determine the point at which a society moves from being industrial to postindustrial. According to Lasch (1972:36), a "Post-industrial society may be said to come into being when capital accumulation has reached the point where scarcity is no longer a social problem—that is, when the industrial system has developed the capacity to satisfy all the basic human needs." Although this capacity has been developed in the advanced industrial countries, it has not yet been fully applied to meet the needs of all persons. As White and Sjoberg (1972) pointed out, many service organizations tend to perpetuate the existing distribution of income and wealth: "Lower-class or disadvantaged clients constantly encounter highly complex rules they do not understand, for they are the ones with the least knowledge of the system."

For Bell (1973:36), the major changes in a postindustrial society occur along the following dimensions:

(1) Economic sector: the change from a goods-producing to a service economy;

(2) Occupational distribution: the preeminence of the professional and technical class;

(3) Axial principle: the centrality of theoretical knowledge as the source of innovation and of policy formulation for the society;

(4) Future orientation: the control of technology and technological assessment;

(5) Decision-making: the creation of a new intellectual technology.

Again, according to these dimensions, the major industrial countries have not yet fully completed the transition from industrial to postindustrial society, which is also indicated by Bell's choice of the title *The Coming of Post-industrial Society* (1973).

One main problem with the postindustrialist perspective (for which Bell's work is the intellectually most stimulating illustration) is its conception within a technocratic framework (Touraine, 1977: 110). As Gartner and Riessman (1974) pointed out:

> There is considerable overlap between Bell's formulation and ours. In essence, it seems to us that he stops short of major developments that are occurring. We are suggesting that the functions that Bell focuses upon are those of a neo-capitalist system in whose womb a new service society is growing. The new service society is not developing in a vacuum; it is emerging in a neo-capitalist industrial context.
>
> It is this dialectic interaction that Bell fails to take into account. In his formulation, the action is largely going one way from the technical structure to the relations of production to the state. But the state may not primarily reflect the knowledge, people, or be "the executive committee of the ruling class," or represent the people; it may represent all three as a battleground for new dimensions of the class struggle.

It is clear, by all accounts of the nature of a postindustrial or service society, that there is no service revolution that would be comparable to the industrial revolution. The latter meant a fundamental change in the relationships between capital, labor, and commodities that led to a new constellation of social classes and gave rise to capitalism. The capitalist mode of production, to be sure, existed already in medieval Europe (Hodgett, 1971; Braudel, 1974; Hobsbawm, 1975) but the industrial revolution enabled its permeation throughout most branches of economic activity. This situation has not changed much in today's advanced capitalist countries; on the contrary, as was noted earlier, some have argued that the shift in the industry structure of employment towards services has resulted in the final penetration of the capitalist mode of production into *all* economic activities (Mandel, 1968; 1972; Braverman, 1974). The growth of service industries in these countries, so far at least, has not altered the fact that most workers have no control over their labor. Although their wages have markedly risen above the subsistence level, very few workers are able to accumulate capital.

But the continuation of the capitalist mode of production in the emerging service economies of the major industrial countries should not imply that the growth of service industries remains without consequences for the social organization of these societies. Social changes linked to the sectoral transformation can be detected; some of which are just emerging while others are already more clearly visible. It is hoped that by calling attention to a few of these trends, future research in these areas will permit a clearer understanding of the differences between industrial and service societies than what we have today. That task becomes even more challenging when one considers that industrial societies themselves differ in many ways (see Dore's (1973) important book *British Factory—Japanese Factory* for a good illustration of these differences), and that for the same reasons, service societies are not likely to be any more similar to each other. To the extent that there are some basic differences between agricultural and industrial societies, some general characteristics of service societies can be expected. It is in the light of this context that the following trends in the advanced industrial countries are addressed.

How Has the Occupational Structure Been Affected
by the Sectoral Transformation?

Up to this point, the discussion has centered exclusively on the industry structure of employment and its changes during the past 50 years. However, there exists a close relationship between the industry structure and the occupational distribution of the work force. In an agriculturally oriented economy, for example, most workers will be in farm-related occupations. As agriculture declines in terms of employment, the occupations of farmers and farm laborers will also become less prominent. In contrast, social and producer services require a large proportion of professional and clerical skills. In the United States in 1970, professionals made up almost one-third of total employment in social services, and clerical workers accounted for two of every five workers in producer services (Browning and Singelmann, 1975:119). Thus, as employment shifts into these two service sectors, white-collar occupations can be expected to gain in importance. The experience of the advanced industrial countries is consistent with this expectation. Data for the United States show, for example, that during the 1960s, the white-collar occupations and service workers expanded their shares of total employment, and the shares of *all* other occupations declined. By the end of that decade, clerical workers had replaced operatives as the largest occupational category. Thus, professionals, clerical workers, and service workers emerge as the most dynamic occupational categories in a service society.

While the growth of these occupations is fairly well documented, a closer inspection of the industry-occupation relationship yields some very interesting results. It can be argued that changes in the occupational structure come about as the result of two types of shifts: (1) the sectoral transformation of employment and (2) shifts in material technology, organization of work, and demands for different quality of work within industries. Studies have shown that the industry shifts are the primary source of occupational changes. In the United States between 1960 and 1970, industry shifts explained two-thirds of all changes in the occupational structure (Browning and Singelmann, 1975:137), and effects of similar magnitudes were found for the United States between 1950 and 1960 (U.S. Department of Labor, 1973) and for Germany during the 1950-1967 period *(Institut für Arbeitsmarkt- und Berufsforschung,* 1973). But most important of all, these studies showed that the proportionate increase of professional positions was almost exclusively due to the shift in the industry structure of employment. In fact, had employment in the United States during the 1960s not shifted towards those industries with a higher demand for professional labor, these positions would have declined in relative terms.

These studies make it clear that the amount of structural mobility (i.e., the upgrading of the work force) in advanced industrial countries is closely linked to the shift from agricultural to transformative industries and, most of all, to social services. However, these findings also imply that at the time when the transformation begins to slow down and comes to a halt, there will be much less additional structural upward mobility. Thus, we should not expect the increase in the number of the higher-status positions to continue at the same rate that was observed in the past.

This outlook has very serious implications for individual mobility and for further improvements in the employment situation of women and minorities. As long as the whole labor force became upgraded, the chances for individual upward mobility were reasonably good, and the integration of women and minorities was relatively costless to the traditional holders of the higher status positions (white males) because the pool of desirable positions continuously increased. But as the structural shifts diminish, individual mobility will more likely become a zero-sum situation. It seems that the growing concern with affirmative action programs is a first sign that this trend has already begun.

Does a Service Economy Improve
the Conditions of Work?

Bell (1973), observing the growth of professional and technical positions in modern industrial countries, argued that the "knowledge" industries, including professionals and technocrats, will play a leading role in a postindustrial society. It has been estimated, for example, that in the United States the quantity of capital and labor have been accounting for a decreasing share of total output during the twentieth century, whereas the increasing balance is explained by "knowledge"—as it manifests itself in new forms of work organization and material technology.

These changes raise fundamental questions about the quality of work in a service society. What is the proportion of privileged positions? Will labor become more creative? Will there be less alienation? Are workers going to be more satisfied with their jobs? Obviously, the scope of these questions is much too broad to permit a full examination of the issues here. Most signs, however, suggest that the quality of work in a service society will be much less different from that of industrial societies than had been previously assumed, although there are some important trends that have to be addressed.

A few years ago, the Department of Health, Education, and Welfare created a special task force to examine the situation of work in the United States. In its report *Work in America* (Upjohn Institute, 1973; see also the commissioned research papers in O'Toole, 1975), the task force concluded:

> [A] significant number of American workers are dissatisfied with the quality of their working lives. Dull, repetitive, seemingly meaningless tasks, offering little challenge or autonomy, are causing discontent among workers at all occupational levels. . . .
> As a result, the productivity of the workers is low—as measured by absenteeism, turnover rates, wildcat strikes, sabotage, poor-quality products, and a reluctance by workers to commit themselves to their work tasks (Upjohn Institute, 1973:XV-XVI).

These conclusions, of course, leave the possibility open that without the shift toward service employment, the conditions of work would be even worse. The finding, for example, that discontent exists in all occupational levels does not imply the degree of discontent to be the same in all groups.

However, this possibility has been challenged by Mandel (1968; 1972), Heilbroner (1976), and most of all, Braverman (1974). In his impressive and stimulating book *Labor and Monopoly Capitalism: The Degradation of Work in the Twentieth Century,* Braverman argues that the shift of employment towards service industries has not improved the position of the workers but has instead resulted in a growing number of workers being employed by capital, and thereby, increasing their dependency on the capitalist mode of production. Most workers in service industries, according to Braverman, perform tasks that are qualitatively not much different from the work in goods-producing industries. Focussing on clerical employment and service workers, he shows how office organization and other forms of scientific management of work have further increased the detailed division of labor within the work force. The result of these trends is a closely supervised worker who performs a fragmented task requiring very few skills. Worse yet, the median wages of these workers fall increasingly behind the wages of the white-collar occupations of the goods-producing sector.

Braverman's arguments are very persuasive and cannot be ignored by any means. The greater part of employment in service industries is far away from the situation of meaningful and creative labor that was envisioned by Mandel (1968:206) for a postindustrial society. The nature of most service industries in their present form only reflect the continued attempt of capital to bring an ever increasing share of employment under its control. Related to this are the attempts to fragmentize service work far enough so that its individual components can be standardized and subjected to precise measurements of efficiency and productivity, because the basic aim of most of these services remains the generation of more capital.

In sum, the sectoral transformation has not altered the basic character of work as alienated labor; this condition of labor is the very basis of capitalism. A large part of employment in services is not much different from work in other industries, and some segments of this employment have replaced the unskilled industrial laborer as the least desirable, and least remunerated, worker.

But Braverman's findings do not completely negate the importance of the growth of services for the quality of work. First, the movement of employment into service industries—and particularly into social services—has resulted in expanded opportunities for creative work. Also, while there is a clearly discernible attempt to standardize work even in social services, many areas of employment still evade these attempts, and, by and large, the degree of autonomy of service employment remains higher. Even those service workers who have relatively low occupational status and little authority within their organization (e.g., welfare workers) maintain a certain degree of control over the scheduling of their work. Second, the nature of services that are provided by an organization can make a difference in the way a worker evaluates his or her position. For example, medical assistants might have a more positive attitude toward their work than, say, cashiers in a bank, because they can view their activities in the context of assisting the well-being of other individuals. Third, many services permit a greater degree of part-time work compared to manufacturing industries. Despite the fact that many persons are forced to work fewer hours than they wish, and that some are compelled to work split shifts (as in restaurants), there exists a large labor-force group that voluntarily works less than the standard work week. Without the opportunity for this type of work in services, the labor force participation rate would probably be substantially lower.

The issues raised here can be empirically answered. What is particularly needed are comparative studies of similar occupations across different industries in order to isolate the industry effect on work, both in terms of a worker's attitude toward work and with regard to the objective conditions of labor.

Does the Sectoral Transformation Lead To New Social Classes and Alliances?

A few years ago Touraine (1971:81) argued that our understanding of economic progress in advanced industrial countries benefits more from an examination of "productivity, efficiency, the rationality of educational policies, land management, the organization of communications and authority in large organizations" than from an analysis of "the traditional production factors capital, labor, and land." And he went on to say that "under these conditions, the idea of two basic classes that constitute separate milieux, one reduced to subsistence, the other to managing surpluses, loses its importance." Although the works by Aronowitz (1974) and Levison (1975), with their emphasis on the homogeneity of the working class, challenge Touraine's thesis, the sectoral transformation of the labor force brings with it new social dynamics, the relationships of which do not fit neatly into a two-class model. If the postindustrial society is defined as "the site of new powers and conflicts," as Touraine (1977:110) argues, the task has to be to identify the basis of this power, its control, and the antagonisms between the different sectors of society.

This task has been addressed by Gartner and Riessman (1974) who note the emergence of three social strata in a service society:

> We believe that it is possible to formulate the concomitant and overlapping existence of three strata within our overall society. On the one hand, there is the old industrial sector composed largely of upper-working class and middle-class people, many of whom live in middle America, and whose cultural traditions emphasize authority, respect, puritanism, old-style individualism, nationalism, security, and so on.
>
> Then there is the neo-industrial group referred to by Bell and the post-industrialists. These are the higher-level technicians, managers, engineers, scientists, and research specialists, who are critical of the development of advanced modern capitalism. For the most part, they have been well coopted for capitalist goals of productivity, accumulation, profit expansion, growth, power. They are an educated elite, while they to some extent have some tension with the traditional capitalist forms that Bell and Galbraith and other imply are somewhat restrictive, they nevertheless have been well rewarded by the system, in no way feel disenfranchised or deprived—a neces-

sary characteristic of any vanguard. To some extent they have developed a whole series of new values and cultures, particularly around rational administration, management, organization, merit, credentials, efficiency, creativity, relative autonomy, and a wide variety of educationally related values.

The third group, we believe, derives from the consumer-service base that is emerging in our society, from the new importance of the consumer and the significance of the services, particularly the human services. The groups involved here are by no means homogeneous— they include the women, students, minorities, service workers, some of the educated affluents, particularly those involved in or related to the professions but less involved in industry, management, research, engineering, and science.

It must be remembered that all three groups are enveloped by the basic neocapitalist frame and this conditions their roles, functions, and values. While there may be important strains or tensions deriving from some of the developing groups, they nevertheless are basically contained by the overall system and its present power.

Two main problems exist in Gartner and Riessman's (1974) treatment of classes in a service society. First, their main emphasis is on the "human" services (which largely correspond to the social services sector used here) with their provider-client relationship. Although this specific focus represents an improvement over the undifferentiated view of services, it simultaneously neglects to take the social dynamics in the other service sectors into account. Second, the three groups identified by Gartner and Riessman (1974) are, as they themselves acknowledge, not mutually exclusive, nor do they exhaust the totality of positions in society. The vagueness of the definitions, moreover, would make it extremely difficult to empirically investigate the social relationships between these groups.

Gartner and Riessman (1974), however, bring one very important aspect of a service economy to light with their discussion of the third group deriving "from the consumer-service base." The growth of this sector makes it possible that an increasing share of the economy can potentially be controlled through alliances and coalitions of interest groups, all of which have a vested interest in the expansion of social services. Poor people, for example, because of the benefits that these services might promise to them, and highly educated middle-class persons because these services offer them employment and political opportunities. These coalitions can include groups of quite disparate socioeconomic status, and they can shift from one issue to the next, depending on the interests of the groups involved. The work of environmental and consumer-oriented organizations, and that of Common Cause, demonstrate that a substantial amount of control over policy formulation can indeed be gained through the various alliances.

Some time ago Dahrendorf (1959,1967) developed the concept of a *service* class. He argued that "a theory of class based on the division of society into owners and non-owners of means of production loses its analytical value as soon as legal ownership and factual control are separated" (1959:136). He therefore, "derived classes from positions in associations coordinated by authority and defined them by the 'characteristic' of participation in or exclusion from the exercise of authority" (1959:151). Accordingly, the service class is made up by those who are in positions to exercise authority in their organizations (1967:315).

Following Dahrendorf's approach, Hardin (1976:149) attempted to estimate the size of the service class in modern industrial societies: "To ascertain the membership of the service class in a nation, we would need occupational data which indicated authority relationships." Using the occupational groups "professional, technical, and related workers" and "administrative, executive, and managerial workers" (groups 0 and 1, respectively, of the International Standard Classification of Occupations), he calculates the size of the service class around 1960 for West Germany, the United Kingdom, and France as being 10-12 percent of the total labor force, 16 percent for Canada, and 19 percent for the United States. However, these two occupational groups are only very crude indicators of the service class, because the degree of authority exercised by their members varies widely. The managerial category, for example, includes self-employed proprietors of small stores as well as the general managers of large corporations.

The task asked for by Dahrendorf cannot be accomplished with the use of census data because they do not offer any information about the position of workers in their organizations with respect to authority and autonomy.

One of the most interesting approaches to class in advanced capitalist societies to date has been developed by Wright (see e.g., Wright and Perrone, 1977). He acknowledges that besides the central classes of bourgeoisie and proletariat, there exist additional groups in contemporary society that occupy contradictory class locations. These include the petty bourgeoisie, managers, and semiautonomous workers. Although Wright did not have adequate data at his disposal to empirically estimate the class structure of society, he was able to arrive at some approximations of the relative size of each class. The results show that the two largest classes today are the proletariat and managers. Employers (bourgeoisie) and the petty bourgeosie (which combined make up the self-employed) account for less than 15 percent of total employment, reflecting the continuous decline of self-employment in advanced industrial societies.

Combining the approach to social classes with the industry-occupation shifts discussed earlier in this chapter, it was possible to assess the relationship between the sectoral transformation and changes in the class structure for the 1960-1970 period in the United States (Singelmann and Wright, 1978). Although the results are only crude approximations, for the inadequacy of the data required some rather sweeping assumptions, they nevertheless suggest two counteracting tendencies. One trend is the growing proletarianization within industries. But this trend is masked, and partly offset, by the sectoral transformation which disfavored the expansion of proletarian positions and tended to inflate managerial and semi-autonomous positions. To the extent that the pace of the sectoral transformation is likely to slow down in the near future, the full degree of proletariani-zation in the advanced industrial societies should become evident. These results, obviously, are only one first step toward a more comprehensive investigation of the relationships between industry, occupation, and social class, but they indicate that such an investigation should indeed prove important for an understanding of the current developments.

In addition to the stratification order of a service society in terms of classes, the dimensions of sex and race will have to be added to the analysis. Women have traditionally provided a main source of workers in the various service industries (except in producer services where their disproportionate representation is of more recent origin) and this relative concentration of female employment in services has further increased (Singelmann, 1974). As recently as 1960 over one-half of all black female workers were employed in personal services in the United States, with 37 percent in domestic service alone.

While the dimension of race is more important in the United States than in the West European countries (with the exception of Great Britain), the emergence of service economies in Western Europe has to be examined in connection with the problem of foreign workers. Until the economic crisis of the 1970s France and, particularly, West Germany had a great demand for foreign labor, because the supply of domestic workers was insufficient. This situation resulted in part from the economic policies in these countries to invest largely in their own country, rather than abroad, and to bring in cheap labor from the poorer countries around the Mediterranean.

With the economic crisis of the 1970s, however, the transformative industries in Europe, which traditionally are very export-oriented, were forced to shrink their employment rolls because of lowered demand both domestically and from abroad. In West Germany, for example, because foreign workers were predominantly employed in manufacturing, rather than in services, they did not receive renewal of their contracts. Combined with the suspension of new foreign recruits and incentives to those foreign workers with valid contracts to return home, the total number of foreign workers in West Germany sank dramatically since the early 1970s. Most of those remaining today have the option of staying as long as they wish, either because of their marital status or sufficiently long tenure in the past. Thus, the sectoral transformation in the European countries is tied to the role of foreign labor in their economies.*

Finally, a full understanding of the sectoral transformation, and particularly the growth of social services, must take into account the role of the state. Demographic changes—such as the baby boom after World War II—do not explain the expansion of these services, not even of education. There can be no doubt that the growth of these services is the result of state policy.** These policies have democratized social services, for they have become available today to a much larger share of the population than in the past. To be sure, socioeconomic differences in mortality still exist, and educational attainment is by no means independent of family origin, but the point here is that in a service society access to social services is becoming more independent of an individual's ability to pay for them. This can be illustrated with a comparison of education in West Germany and the United States. The fact that in the United States in 1970 education accounted for 8.6 percent of total employment, compared to only 3.0 percent in West Germany, says something about the differences between these two countries in the extent and availability of educational services.

The expansion of the social service sector has lead to a substantial shift of economic activities from a market to a nonmarket context. Increasingly, the state sets priorities for consumption by allocating growing parts of salaries and wages, through taxation, to specific programs. In Great Britain, for example, an important element of the just completed three-phase economic recovery program concerned the agreement of the labor unions to wage constraints in return for greater public access to social programs.

---

*Although some parallels exist in the function of foreign labor in Europe with the position of the so-called undocumented workers in the United States, their situation is sufficiently different to warrant a separate analysis.

**Japan is a special case in this respect since its specific form of industrial organization allocates the function of many social services to the level of enterprises (Dore, 1973). See also Tsurutani's (1976) description of "Japan as a postindustrial society."

The growth of social services has also very important repercussions for the expansion of the public sector, because the three largest social services—hospitals, education, and public administration (including postal service)—are overwhelmingly government-run. The growth of social services, therefore, has increased the role of the state as employer. (The role of the state as a direct employer can easily be assessed by differentiating in all 37 industries between public and private employment and those that are self-employed. The indirect role of the state as employer is more difficult to assess, for it refers to the share of employment in all industries that is created by state expenditures.) In the past, governmental employees were considered a relatively conservative work force, but recent strikes by postal workers, teachers, and nurses have shown that these groups increasingly turn towards collective organization in their bargaining attempts. This situation is also reflected in the growing unionization of government employees. In fact, the American Federation of State, County, and Municipal Employees (AFSCME) today is one of the fastest growing unions in the United States. Here and in Canada, this development is fairly recent, but in the European countries unionization of government workers—even including the armed forces—has had a much longer tradition. But in all countries, the trend is toward a direct, and increasing, confrontation between employment groups and the state over wages and salaries, which puts the state increasingly at the center of social conflict.

It has already been stated that the rate of expansion of social services in the advanced industrial countries is likely to slow down, in part because of the size of fiscal deficits characterizing most of their governments. The issue of the future of social services has been placed by Manuel Castells (1978) in its exact dimension:

[Human services] can be used to simply absorb surplus population, or used as pork-barrel policies by local governments, or they can be the consequences of successful pressure from the grassroots. In terms of new jobs and more services, they can be the response to demands

of scientific and technological development or a political trend
toward a welfare state. In short, the development of human services
(which seems to be the hard core of the theory of development
through services) is a *social process* and its evolution and characteristics will be the *result of political conflicts* concerning the political
economy.

Social forecasting bears the risk of mistakes and sometimes
ridicule. It was only forty years ago that for the United States a
maximal population size of 180 million was projected for the year
1970, to be followed by a decline to 76 million. Obviously,
something went wrong. Is the preceding discussion awaiting a
similar fate? I believe not. There are strong signs that the period of
rapid economic growth that began in the 1940s is coming to a halt
in the major industrial countries. The recent economic summit
meeting of the leaders of these seven countries in London in May
1977, made it clear that these countries are facing the needs of a
major reorientation in their pattern of consumption and in their
relationship with the nations of the Third World. One need not
share the pessimism of some of the recent publications by the
Club of Rome to realize that the availability of energy, water, and
other natural resources can no longer be taken for granted. The
current energy discussion in the United States shows that this
awareness is spreading quickly. As the experience of other highly
industrialized countries shows, a strong economic performance
can be achieved at much lower levels of energy consumption than
is presently the case in the United States. However, it seems that
most proposals that deal with new policies concerning the use of
natural resources ultimately will benefit the further expansion of
services, be it mass transportation, the production of more
durable goods, or even a further shift towards fewer work hours
instead of higher wages. Aside from these trends, there are still
many improvements to be made toward a more equal availability
of social services to all persons. In this sense, the future of today's
major industrial countries belongs to the service society.

APPENDIX A: COUNTRY TABLES

Table A.1: Percentage Distribution of Employment by Industry Sectors and Intermediate Industry Groups, 1920-1970

Sectors and Industries	1920	1930	1940	1950	1960	1970
I. Extractive	28.9	25.4	21.3	14.4	8.1	4.5
(1) Agriculture	26.3	22.9	19.2	12.7	7.0	3.7
(2) Mining	2.6	2.5	2.1	1.7	1.1	0.8
II. Transformative	32.9	31.5	29.8	33.9	35.9	33.1
(3) Construction		6.5	4.7	6.2	6.2	5.8
(4) Food		2.3	2.7	2.7	3.1	2.0
(5) Textile		4.2	2.6	2.2	3.3	3.0
(6) Metal		} 7.7	2.9	3.6	3.9	3.3
(7) Machinery	32.9		2.4	3.7	7.5	8.3
(8) Chemical			1.3	1.5	1.7	1.8	1.6
(9) Misc. manufacturing		9.0	11.8	12.3	8.7	7.7
(10) Utilities		0.6	1.2	1.4	1.4	1.4
III. Distributive Services	18.7	19.6	20.4	22.4	21.9	22.3
(11) Transportation	} 7.6	6.0	4.9	5.3	4.4	3.9
(12) Communication		1.0	0.9	1.2	1.3	1.5
(13) Wholesale	} 11.1	12.6	2.7	3.5	3.6	4.1
(14) Retail		12.6	11.8	12.3	12.5	12.8
IV. Producer Services	2.8	3.2	4.6	4.8	6.6	8.2
(15) Banking		1.3	1.1	1.1	1.6	2.6
(16) Insurance		1.1	1.2	1.4	1.7	1.8
(17) Real Estate		0.6	1.1	1.0	1.0	1.0
(18) Engineering	2.8	–	} 1.3	0.2	0.3	0.4
(19) Accounting		–		0.2	0.3	0.4
(20) Misc. business serv.		0.1		0.6	1.2	1.8
(21) Legal services		–		0.4	0.5	0.5

Table A.1: (Continued)

Sectors and Industries	1920	1930	1940	1950	1960	1970
V. Social Services	8.7	9.2	10.0	12.4	16.3	21.9
(22) Medical services		–	} 2.3	1.1	1.4	2.2
(23) Hospitals		–	2.3	1.8	2.7	3.7
(24) Education		–	3.5	3.8	5.4	8.6
(25) Welfare		–	} 0.9	0.7	1.0	1.2
(26) Nonprofit	8.7	–	0.9	0.3	0.4	0.4
(27) Postal services		0.6	0.7	0.8	0.9	1.0
(28) Government		2.2	2.6	3.7	4.3	4.6
(29) Misc. social serv.		6.3	–	0.1	0.2	0.3
VI. Personal Services	8.2	11.2	14.0	12.1	11.3	10.0
(30) Domestic services		6.5	5.3	3.2	3.1	1.7
(31) Hotels		} 2.9	1.3	1.0	1.0	1.0
(32) Eating and drinking places		2.9	2.5	3.0	2.9	3.3
(33) Repair		–	1.5	1.7	1.4	1.3
(34) Laundry	8.2	–	1.0	1.2	1.0	0.8
(35) Barber and beauty shop		0.9	–	–	0.8	0.9
(36) Entertainment		0.9	0.9	1.0	0.8	0.8
(37) Misc. personal serv.		–	1.6	1.2	0.4	0.3
Total Labor Force	100.2	100.1	100.1	100.0	100.1	100.0

Note: Percentages may not add to one hundred because of rounding.

Table A.2: CANADA: Percentage Distribution of Employment by Industry Sectors and Intermediate Industry Groups, 1921-1971

Sectors and Industries	1921	1931	1941	1951	1961	1971
I. Extractive	36.9	34.4	31.7	21.6	14.7	9.1
(1) Agriculture	35.2	32.5	29.5	19.7	12.8	7.4
(2) Mining	1.6	1.9	2.2	1.9	1.9	1.7
II. Transformative	26.1	24.7	28.2	33.7	31.2	30.0
(3) Construction	9.0	6.8	5.3	6.9	7.0	6.9
(4) Food	1.2	2.2	3.4	3.1	3.7	3.2
(5) Textiles	2.7	2.6	3.7	1.6	1.3	0.9
(6) Metal	} 2.9	1.9	2.3	} 3.9	3.2	1.5
(7) Machinery	2.9	0.7	0.9	3.9	0.8	1.0
(8) Chemical	0.2	0.4	0.8	1.3	1.4	1.0
(9) Misc. manufacturing	10.0	8.6	11.2	15.7	12.6	14.4
(10) Utilities	–	1.5	0.6	1.2	1.1	1.1

Table A.2 (Continued)

Sectors and Industries	1921	1931	1941	1951	1961	1971
III. Distributive Services	19.2	18.4	17.6	21.7	23.9	23.0
(11) Transportation	8.5	7.2	5.8	6.8	6.6	5.4
(12) Communication	–	0.9	0.7	1.1	2.1	2.1
(13) Wholesale trade	} 10.7	1.6	2.4	3.8	4.7	4.5
(14) Retail trade		8.7	8.8	10.1	10.5	11.0
IV. Producer Services	3.7	3.3	2.8	4.0	5.3	7.3
(15) Banking	} 1.2	1.2	0.9	1.3	1.8	2.4
(16) Insurance		1.0	0.9	1.1	} 1.9	} 2.2
(17) Real estate		0.2	0.3	0.4		
(18) Engineering	} 2.3	–	–	0.2	0.4	0.7
(19) Accounting		0.1	0.1	0.2	0.3	0.4
(20) Misc. business serv.		0.4	0.2	0.4	0.5	1.1
(21) Legal services	0.2	0.4	0.3	0.3	0.4	0.5
V. Social Services	7.5	8.9	9.4	11.3	15.3	21.1
(22) Medical, health serv.	} 1.1	1.8	2.2	3.1	0.9	1.0
(23) Hospitals					3.7	4.7
(24) Education	2.0	2.7	2.7	2.9	4.4	7.3
(25) Welfare, religious services	0.9	1.0	0.7	1.1	1.3	1.4
(26) Nonprofit org.	–	–	–	–	–	0.2
(27) Postal services	} 3.0	0.5	0.5	0.6	} 5.1	} 5.4
(28) Government		2.6	2.8	3.4		
(29) Misc. social serv.	0.5	0.3	0.5	0.2	–	–
VI. Personal Services	6.7	10.3	10.3	7.8	9.6	9.5
(30) Domestic service	–	4.2	4.5	1.6	1.6	0.7
(31) Hotels	–	} 2.8	1.6	1.5	} 3.9	1.7
(32) Eating, drinking places	–		1.3	1.6		2.6
(33) Repair service	–	0.5	1.1	1.1	1.1	0.9
(34) Laundry, cleaning, dying	–	0.5	0.5	0.7	0.6	0.5
(35) Barber and beauty shops	–	0.6	0.6	0.5	0.7	0.7
(36) Entertainment, recreation	–	0.4	0.4	0.5	0.6	1.0
(37) Misc. personal serv.	–	1.2	0.2	0.3	1.0	1.5
	100.1	100.0	100.0	100.1	100.0	100.0

Note: Percentages may not add to one hundred because of rounding.

Table A.3: ENGLAND AND WALES: Percentage Distribution of Employment by Industry Sectors and Intermediate Industry Groups, 1921-1971

Sectors and Industries	1921	1931	1951	1961	1971
I. Extractive	14.2	11.8	8.9	6.6	4.2
(1) Agriculture	7.1	6.1	5.0	3.5	2.6
(2) Mining	7.1	5.7	3.9	3.1	1.7
II. Transformative	42.2	39.3	45.4	46.0	43.8
(3) Construction	4.4	5.2	6.5	6.9	7.1
(4) Food	3.3	3.4	3.0	3.0	3.0
(5) Textiles	5.9	5.9	4.5	3.4	2.4
(6) Metal	2.8	2.1	2.7	2.7	2.3
(7) Machinery	1.6	1.4	3.0	3.2	4.8
(8) Chemical	1.2	1.1	2.1	2.3	2.0
(9) Misc. Manufacturing	22.1	19.0	21.9	22.8	20.4
(10) Utilities	1.0	1.3	1.7	1.7	1.6
III. Distributive Services	19.3	21.6	19.2	19.7	17.9
(11) Transportation	7.3	7.0	6.4	5.7	4.8
(12) Communication	–	–	–	–	–
(13) Wholesale	} 12.0	} 14.6	} 12.8	} 14.0	3.4
(14) Retail					9.6
IV. Producer Services	2.6	3.1	3.2	4.5	5.6
(15) Banking	0.8	0.8	0.9	1.2	1.6
(16) Insurance	0.7	0.9	0.9	1.1	1.2
(17) Real estate	–	0.3	0.3	0.3	0.4
(18) Engineering	0.2	0.2	0.2	–	0.4
(19) Accounting	0.0	0.3	0.3	0.4	0.4
(20) Misc. business serv.	0.4	0.2	0.1	1.1	1.0
(21) Legal services	0.4	0.4	0.4	0.4	0.5
V. Social Services	8.9	9.7	12.1	14.1	19.4
(22) Medical, health serv.	} 1.0	} 1.1	} 2.9	} 3.4	0.8
(23) Hospitals					3.1
(24) Education	2.1	2.2	2.4	3.9	5.8
(25) Welfare, religious serv.	0.6	0.6	0.6	0.7	1.0
(26) Nonprofit org.	0.1	0.1	–	0.0	0.2
(27) Postal services	1.1	1.2	1.6	1.6	1.8
(28) Government	3.8	4.3	4.2	4.0	6.0
(29) Misc. social services	0.2	0.2	0.4	0.6	0.6
VI. Personal Services	12.9	14.5	11.3	9.0	9.0
(30) Domestic service	7.5	8.2	2.4	1.6	1.0
(31) Hotels	2.4	2.2	} 4.2	} 2.7	1.6
(32) Eating, drinking places	0.8	1.3			1.0
(33) Repair services	–	–	1.4	1.8	2.1
(34) Laundry, cleaning, dying	0.8	0.9	0.8	0.7	0.4
(35) Barber, beauty shops	0.3	0.5	0.4	0.7	1.1
(36) Entertainment	0.7	0.9	1.1	1.0	1.1
(37) Misc. personal serv.	0.5	0.3	1.0	0.5	0.8
	100.1	100.0	100.1	99.9	99.9

Note: Percentages may not add to one hundred because of rounding.

Table A.4: GERMANY: Percentage Distribution of Employment by Industry Sectors and Intermediate Industry Groups, 1925-1970

Sectors and Industries	1925	1933	1950	1961	1970
I. Extractive	33.5	31.5	16.1	9.0	5.1
(1) Agriculture	30.9	29.1	12.9	6.8	3.8
(2) Mining	2.6	2.4	3.2	2.2	1.3
II. Transformative	38.9	38.3	47.3	51.3	49.0
(3) Construction	5.3	6.1	9.3	8.5	8.0
(4) Food	4.3	5.1	4.6	3.1	3.8
(5) Textiles	3.7	3.5	3.5	5.1	2.2
(6) Metal	3.7	4.5	2.3	3.7	3.7
(7) Machinery	2.9	3.4	3.0	5.0	4.8
(8) Chemical	1.1	1.1	1.7	2.4	2.7
(9) Misc. Manufacturing	17.3	14.0	22.0	22.3	23.0
(10) Utilities	0.6	0.6	0.8	1.2	0.8
III. Distributive Services	11.9	12.8	15.7	16.4	16.9
(11) Transportation	4.0	4.2	5.1	4.5	3.9
(12) Communication	–	–	–	0.5	–
(13) Wholesale trade	} 7.9	8.6	10.6	3.9	4.4
(14) Retail trade				7.5	8.6
IV. Producer Services	2.1	2.7	2.5	4.2	5.1
(15) Banking	0.7	0.6	0.7	1.2	1.7
(16) Insurance	0.4	0.6	0.8	0.7	1.0
(17) Real estate	0.0	0.6	0.1	0.3	0.4
(18) Engineering	0.1	0.1	0.2	0.4	0.6
(19) Accounting	} 0.5	0.3	0.3	1.0	0.7
(20) Misc. business service					
(21) Legal services	0.3	0.6	0.5	0.6	0.8
V. Social Services	6.0	6.8	11.5	12.9	17.4
(22) Medical, health serv.	0.4	} 1.3	2.4	2.5	3.2
(23) Hospital	0.6				
(24) Education	1.1	1.2	1.5	2.1	3.0
(25) Welfare, relig. serv.	0.5	0.8	1.0	0.9	0.4
(26) Nonprofit org.	–	–	–	–	0.4
(27) Postal service	1.1	1.1	1.5	1.7	1.8
(28) Government	2.1	2.2	4.1	5.3	8.6
(29) Misc. social serv.	0.1	0.2	0.6	–	–
VI. Personal Services	7.7	7.8	6.8	6.4	6.5
(30) Domestic	4.4	4.0	3.2	1.5	0.5
(31) Hotels	} 2.1	2.4	2.2	2.6	2.9
(32) Eating, drinking places					
(33) Repair service	–	–	–	–	1.1
(34) Laundry	0.2	–	–	0.6	0.5
(35) Barber, beauty shops	0.4	0.7	0.8	0.9	0.9
(36) Entertainment	0.4	0.5	0.1	–	0.4
(37) Misc. personal serv.	0.1	0.2	0.6	0.8	0.4
	100.1	99.9	99.9	100.2	100.0

Note: Percentages may not add to one hundred because of rounding.

Table A.5: FRANCE: Percentage Distribution of the Labor Force by
Industry Sectors and Intermediate Industry Groups, 1921-1968

Sectors and Industries	1921	1931	1946	1954	1962	1968
I. Extractive	43.6	38.3	40.2	31.9	23.0	17.0
(1) Agriculture	42.4	36.6	38.8	28.6	20.6	15.9
(2) Mining	1.2	1.7	1.4	2.3	2.4	1.1
II. Transformative	29.7	32.8	29.6	35.2	37.7	39.3
(3) Construction	3.0	4.2	5.1	7.4	8.7	10.3
(4) Food	2.3	2.6	2.2	3.2	3.1	3.0
(5) Textiles	9.4	4.4	2.5	6.0	4.9	2.3
(6) Metal	0.6	2.1	} 7.3	0.9	1.1	1.5
(7) Machinery	–	–		0.9	1.2	1.3
(8) Chemical	0.9	1.1	1.1	1.3	1.4	1.5
(9) Misc. manufacturing	13.2	18.3	10.7	14.9	16.3	18.5
(10) Utilities	0.2	0.0	0.6	0.7	0.8	0.8
III. Distributive Services	14.4	13.3	15.1	14.4	16.4	15.5
(11) Transportation	5.6	} 5.1	6.1	4.2	4.3	4.3
(12) Communication	0.7			1.3	1.7	0.1
(13) Wholesale	} 8.1	8.5	9.1	2.3	3.2	3.6
(14) Retail				6.5	7.3	7.5
IV. Producer Services	1.6	2.1	1.9	2.7	3.2	5.5
(15) Banking	0.6	0.9	1.2	0.8	1.1	2.0
(16) Insurance	0.2	0.3	0.4	0.5	0.7	0.8
(17) Real Estate	0.0	0.0	0.0	0.4	0.2	0.4
(18) Engineering			–			0.3
(19) Accounting	} 0.5	0.7	–	0.9	1.1	1.6
(20) Misc. bs. serv.			–			
(21) Legal services	0.3	0.3	0.3	–	–	0.4
V. Social Services	5.3	6.1	6.8	9.4	12.3	14.8
(22) Medical, health serv.	} 0.9	1.1	1.2	2.2	2.9	1.0
(23) Hospitals						2.2
(24) Education	1.3	1.4	1.5	2.4	3.5	4.4
(25) Welfare, religious serv.	0.5	0.5	0.7	0.6	1.1	1.1
(26) Nonprofit org.	–	–	–	–	1.0	0.7
(27) Postal service	} 2.3	2.8	3.2	4.0	3.4	1.8
(28) Government						3.3
(29) Misc. social serv.	0.2	0.2	0.1	0.2	0.4	0.0
VI. Personal Services	5.6	7.2	6.4	7.4	7.4	7.9
(30) Domestic service	3.7	3.8	1.3	3.1	3.0	2.7
(31) Hotels				1.5	1.6	0.9
(32) Eating, drinking places	} 1.5	2.8	1.4	1.4	1.2	1.8

Table A.5 (Continued)

Sectors and Industries	1921	1931	1946	1954	1962	1968
(33) Repair serv.	–	–	–	–	0.3	1.1
(34) Laundry	–	–	0.2	} 1.0		0.5
(35) Barber, beauty shops	0.3	–	–		1.2	0.7
(36) Entertainment	0.1	0.2	0.3	0.4	0.2	0.2
(37) Misc. personal serv.	0.0	0.5	3.2	–	0.0	0.0
	100.2	99.8	100.0	100.0	100.0	100.0

Note: Percentages may not add to one hundred because of rounding.

Table A.6: ITALY: Percentage Distribution of the Labor Force by Industry Sectors and Intermediate Industry Groups, 1921-1961

Sectors and Industries	1921	1931	1951	1961
I. Extractive	57.1	48.1	42.9	29.8
(1) Agriculture	56.7	47.7	42.5	29.1
(2) Mining	0.4	0.4	0.4	0.7
II. Transformative	24.2	29.2	32.0	40.0
((3) Construction	4.0	6.0	7.6	12.0
(4) Food	1.2	1.5	2.4	2.4
(5) Textile	3.2	4.2	3.7	3.4
(6) Metal	1.8	} 4.4	1.2	1.5
(7) Machinery	1.5		1.4	1.8
(8) Chemical	0.4	1.0	1.1	1.4
(9) Misc. Manufacturing	11.8	11.3	13.9	16.9
(10) Utilities	0.3	0.6	0.5	0.6
III. Distributive Services	8.6	10.1	10.6	13.1
(11) Transportation	3.9	4.2	3.4	4.1
(12) Communication	0.4	0.5	0.6	0.8
(13) Wholesale	} 4.3	5.4	1.2	1.4
(14) Retail			5.4	6.7
IV. Producer Services	1.3	1.8	1.9	2.0
(15) Banking	} 0.2	0.5	0.8	0.9
(16) Insurance				0.2
(17) Real Estate		} 0.1	} 0.1	0.0
(18) Engineering				} 0.3
(19) Accounting	} 0.8	1.0	0.7	
(20) Misc. business service				0.2
(21) Legal services	0.2	0.2	0.3	0.4
V. Social Services	4.1	5.2	7.9	9.4
(22) Medical, health service	} 0.6	0.8	1.1	0.7
(23) Hospitals				0.9

Table A.6: (Continued)

Sectors and Industries	1921	1931	1951	1961
(24) Education	1.0	1.1	2.0	2.7
(25) Welfare, relig. serv.	0.6	0.7	1.2	0.2
(26) Nonprofit org.	–	0.1	0.1	–
(27) Postal service	} 1.3	2.1	3.4	4.8
(28) Government				
(29) Misc. social service	0.6	0.3	0.1	–
VI. Personal Services	4.6	5.6	4.7	5.9
(30) Domestic service	2.4	3.2	2.2	2.2
(31) Hotels	0.2	0.6	} 1.4	0.7
(32) Eating, drinking places	0.8	0.7		1.4
(33) Repair service	–	–	–	–
(34) Laundry	0.3	0.2	0.1	0.2
(35) Barber, beauty shops	0.4	0.7	0.6	0.9
(36) Entertainmnet	0.0	0.1	0.3	0.3
(37) Misc. personal service	0.5	0.1	0.1	0.2
	99.9	100.0	100.0	100.2

Note: Percentages may not add to one hundred due to rounding.

Table A.7: JAPAN: Percentage Distribution of Employment by Industry Sectors and Intermediate Industry Groups, 1920-1970

Industries and Sectors	1920	1930	1940	1950	1960	1970
I. Extractive	56.3	50.9	46.3	50.3	34.1	19.6
(1) Agriculture	54.9	49.9	44.0	48.6	32.9	19.4
(2) Mining	1.5	1.0	2.2	1.7	1.2	0.3
II. Transformative	19.8	19.8	24.9	21.0	28.5	34.2
(3) Construction	2.7	3.3	3.0	4.3	6.2	7.6
(4) Food	2.0	1.8	1.4	2.2	2.1	2.1
(5) Textiles	5.0	4.8	3.9	3.1	3.2	2.7
(6) Metal	1.0	0.8	1.4	1.6	2.9	1.5
(7) Machinery	0.4	0.7	2.9	1.6	3.1	4.9
(8) Chemical	0.4	0.6	1.1	1.2	1.2	1.3
(9) Misc. Mfg.	7.8	7.4	10.9	6.4	9.2	13.5
(10) Utilities	0.3	0.4	0.4	0.6	0.5	0.6
III. Distributive Services	12.5	15.6	15.2	14.6	18.6	22.5
(11) Transportation	3.5	3.2	3.4	3.5	4.0	5.1
(12) Communication	0.4	0.7	0.9	1.0	1.1	1.2
(13) Wholesale	} 8.5	11.6	10.9	2.3	4.7	6.1
(14) Retail				7.8	8.9	10.2
IV. Producer Services	0.8	0.9	1.2	1.5	2.9	5.1
(15) Banking	0.4	0.5	0.6	0.7	1.2	1.4

Table A.7: (Continued)

Industries and Sectors	1920	1930	1940	1950	1960	1970
(16) Insurance	0.1	0.2	0.3	0.2	0.5	0.7
(17) Real estate	–	–	0.1	0.0	0.2	0.5
(18) Engineering	0.0	–				0.5
(19) Accounting	–	–	} 0.3	0.3	1.0	0.2
(20) Misc. bs. serv.	0.2	0.2				1.7
(21) Legal services	0.1	0.0	0.0	0.2	0.1	0.1
V. Social Services	4.9	5.5	6.0	7.2	8.3	10.1
(22) Medical, health serv.	0.4	0.3	0.4	} 1.1	0.3	0.2
(23) Hospital	0.3	0.5	0.7		1.3	1.8
(24) Education	0.9	1.3	1.5	2.2	2.4	2.7
(25) Welfare, relig. serv.	0.6	0.6	0.6	0.3	0.6	0.7
(26) Nonprofit org.	0.1	–	0.7	0.2	0.2	0.5
(27) Postal Service (28) Government	} 2.2	2.5	1.9	3.3	3.1	3.3
(29) Misc. social services	0.3	0.3	0.3	0.1	0.6	0.9
VI. Personal Services	5.7	7.3	6.3	5.3	7.6	8.5
(30) Domestic serv.	2.5	2.7	2.2	0.8	0.7	0.3
(31) Hotel	0.5	0.5	0.5	0.5	0.8	0.9
(32) Eating, drinking places	1.4	2.4	1.8	1.1	2.2	3.1
(33) Repair service	0.0	0.1	–	0.9	0.7	0.9
(34) Laundry	0.1	0.2	0.2	0.2	0.4	0.5
(35) Barber, beauty shops	0.5	0.7	0.6	0.6	1.1	1.1
(36) Entertainment	0.4	0.3	0.8	0.5	0.7	0.7
(37) Misc. personal serv.	0.2	0.3	0.3	0.7	1.0	1.0
	100.0	100.0	99.9	99.9	100.0	100.0

Note: Percentages may not add to one hundred because of rounding.

Sources for Appendix A

United States:

1920–U. S. Department of Commerce, Bureau of the Census. *14th Census of the United States, 1920.* Volume IV, Table 2.

1930–U. S. Department of Commerce, Bureau of the Census. *U.S. Census of Population, 1930.* Volume V - General Report on Occupations. Washington, D.C.: Chapter 7, Table 1. U.S. Government Printing Office, 1933.

1940–U. S. Department of Commerce, Bureau of the Census. *U. S. Census of Population, 1940.* Volume III, Part 1, Table 74. Washington, D.C.: Government Printing Office, 1943.

1950–U. S. Department of Commerce, Bureau of the Census. *U. S. Census of Population, 1950.* Volume IV, Special Reports, Part 1, Chapter D: Industrial Characteristics. Table 1. Washington, D. C.: U. S. Government Printing Office, 1955.

1960–U. S. Department of Commerce, Bureau of the Census. *U. S. Census of Population, 1960.* Subjects Reports: Industrial Characteristics. Final Report PC(2)-7F, Table 2. Washington, D. C.: U. S. Government Printing Office, 1967.

1970–1/100 Public Use Sample.

Canada:

1921–Department of Trade and Commerce. *Sixth Census of Canada, 1921.* Volume IV, Table 1.

1931–Department of Trade and Commerce. *Seventh Census of Canada, 1931.* Volume VII, Table 56.

1941–Department of Trade and Commerce. *Eighth Census of Canada, 1941.* Volume VII, Table 17.

1951–Department of Trade and Commerce. *Ninth Census of Canada, 1951.* Volume IV, Table 16.

1961–Dominion Bureau of Statistics. *1961. Census of Canada.* Bulletin 3.2-1, Table 1.

1971–Ministry of Industry, Trade and Commerce. *1971 Census of Canada.* Industries: Table 2.

England and Wales:

1921–General Register Office. *Census of England and Wales, 1921.* Table 1. London: H.M.S.O., 1925.

1931–General Register Office. *Census of England and Wales, 1931.* Table 1. London: H.M.S.O., 1934.

1951–General Register Office. *Census of England and Wales, 1961.* Industry Tables, Part I. Pp. XLVII-LI. London: H.M.S.O., 1965.

1961–General Register Office. *Census of England and Wales, 1961.* Industry Tables, Part I. Pp. XLVII-LI. London: H.M.S.O., 1965.

1971–General Register Office. *Census of England and Wales, 1971.* 1% Sample. Industry Tables. London: H.M.S.O., 1974

Germany:

1925–Statistik des Deutschen Reiches, Band 402. Teil 2, pp. 244-409. Berlin, 1929.

1933–Statistik des Deutschen Reiches, Band 470. *Die Hauptergebnisse der Volks-, Berufs- and Betriebszählung im Deutschen Reich (einschl. Saarland), 1933 and 1935.* Heft 2. Berlin, 1937.

1950–Statistik der Bundesrepublik Deutschland, Band 36. *Die berufliche und soziale Gliederung der Bevölkerung der Bundesrepublik Deutschland, 1950.* Teil I, Heft 1, Table 1. Wiesbaden, 1954.

1961–Statistiches Bundesamt Wiesbaden. *Volks- und Berufszählung vom 6. Juni 1961.* Volume 12, Table 4. Wiesbaden, 1967.

1970–Statistisches Bundesamt Wiesbaden. Volkszählung vom 27. Mai 1970. Heft 17: *Erwerbstätige in wirtschaftlicher Gliederung nach Wochenarbeitszeit und weiterer Tätigkeit.* Stuttgart: Kohlhammer, 1974.

France:
1921–Ministere du Travail. *Résultats Statistiques du Recensement Général de la Population, 1921.* Volume I, Part 3, Tables 5 and 7. Paris: Imprimerie Nationale, 1927.
1931–Ministere du Travail. *Résultats Statistiques du Recensement Général de la Population, 1931.* Volume III, Table 7. Paris: Imprimerie Nationale, 1935.
1946–Institut Nationale. *Recensement Général de la Population, 1946.* Volume III, pp. 54 and 364-385. Paris: Imprimerie Nationale, 1952.
1954–Institut Nationale. *Recensement Général de la Population, 1954.* Volume IV. Paris: Imprimerie Nationale, 1958.
1962–Institut Nationale. *Recensement Général de la Population, 1962.* Volume V. Paris: Imprimerie Nationale, 1964.
1968–Institut Nationale. *Recensement Général de la Population, 1968.* Paris: Imprimerie Nationale, 1970.

Italy:
1921–Instituto Centrale di Statistica, 1928: Volume XIX, Table 22.
1931–Instituto Centrale di Statistica, 1935: Volume IV, Part 2, Table 11.
1951–Instituto Centrale di Statistica, 1957: Volume IV, Table 9.
1961–Instituto Centrale di Statistica, 1965: Volume VI, Table 8.

Japan:
1920–Bureau of Statistics. *1970 Population Census of Japan.* Reference Report Series No. 3: Comparison of Employed Persons by Industry in the Population Censuses, 1920 through 1970. Table 1. Tokyo, 1973.
1930–Same as for 1920.
1940–Same as for 1920.
1950–Bureau of Statistics. *Population Census of 1950.* Volume V, Table 3. Tokyo, 1954.
1960–Bureau of Statistics. *1960 Population Census of Japan.* Volume II, Part 3, Table 5. Tokyo, 1962.
1970–Bureau of Statistics. *Comparison of Employed Persons by Industry in the Population Censuses, 1920 through 1970.* Table 1. Tokyo, 1973.

APPENDIX B: MEASUREMENT OF THE LABOR FORCE

Throughout the previous chapters the term labor force has been employed without any further explanation of its definition and limitation. Clearly, people in the labor force all have in common that they work. However, work can be performed in many different forms and with equally many purposes. To merely refer to work as the common characteristic of members of the labor force would be vague and misleading. This chapter, therefore, discusses the various definitions of the labor force employed by national census bureaus, and their changes over time. In addition, the limitations of this concept for a comprehensive study of economic activities in a society are pointed out.

THE NATURE OF WORK

Firth (1948:94) observed that the term work is commonly used in two senses: "The first and broader sense is that of purposive activity entailing the expenditure of energy at some sacrifice of pleasure. The second and narrower sense is that of income-producing activity." To speak about work, however, necessarily implies the existence of activities that are not work. Many difficulties exist in determining where work ends and where work-free (leisure) time begins, and even Firth's two kinds of work overlap each other. In any case, work is not restricted to an activity "on the job", as can be illustrated by the following continuum of activities ranging from work-free behavior to work (see Figure B.1).

As can be seen from this illustration, it is almost impossible to draw the exact line between work and no work. Household activities, of course, must be classified as work but even many hobby activities can result in much labor; their products (such as furniture or handicrafts) often do not differ very much from those produced within a more organized business establishment. Only certain forms of leisure, then, may qualify as no work at all, but even here exceptions come to mind.

This brief discussion may suffice to demonstrate that work encompasses many different meanings and dimensions. This has been aptly summarized by Steiner (1947:116): "There is no activity as such which could not be labour at one time and something quite different at another. We make a distinction on the basis of the cash nexus and translate the latter into more economic terms."

In the course of economic development a change in the prevailing form of work in a society seems to occur. In tradi-

Figure B.1: Nonwork - Work Continuum of Activities

Nonwork

leisure activity

hobby activity

household activity

self-employment

salaried or wage employment

Work

tional societies living off hunting and gathering, most labor involves domestic and agricultural work (which in a sense is self-employment). An industrial society requires work that is regulated by a certain degree of organization. Concomitantly, independent labor (self-employment) becomes increasingly dependent (wage and salary employment). This transition of the nature of labor led to the concept of the economically active population.

THE ECONOMICALLY ACTIVE POPULATION

The emphasis on the relationship between work and monetary rewards has resulted in the situation where the official national statistics of the working population includes only persons whose labor can be expressed in economic terms. According to that definition, labor has a monetary value which can be exchanged for cash or commodities. Going back to the illustration in Figure B.1, of the five types of activities listed only self-employment and, wage and salary employment are included in the economically active population. While wage and salary employment clearly fits the exchange model, self-employment differs from it to the extent that the exchange of labor and rewards is indirect. The relationship between labor and monetary rewards of a self-employed artisan, for example, is intermediated by the product that he sells. On the other hand, since in modern economies self-employment exists primarily in service industries where labor and product coincide, self-employment, too, is consistent with the exchange model.

Besides these two forms of labor, most countries include unpaid family members in the economically active population. A family member helping without pay on the family-owned farm, for example, would be classified as economically active. The majority of this type of work is mostly found in agriculture, but other industries such as retail trade and some personal services utilize unpaid family members as well. In contrast, the nature of most social services (which are often governmental) or transformative industries with their strict scheduling requirements is not conducive to this type of work. In the course of economic development, therefore, this labor category diminishes greatly.

As a result of this emphasis on the exchange model, the term economically active population refers to only a segment of work that is being performed in a society. This limitation can be demonstrated by household work. In the case where a person employs the services of someone else to do the necessary domestic chores, this work would be classified as economically active, for a service is being exchanged for pay. However, should the employer and the employee become married (which history shows us to be not that uncommon), and their division of labor is being continued, the same household work would suddenly cease to be economically active.

The concept of the economically active population fits some societies better than others. It can generally be said that the exchange requirement underlying this concept prevents us from applying it to studies of work in preindustrial societies. However, as the example of household work illustrates, the utility of that concept, moreover, is also limited as far as the investigation of the female labor force is concerned because females perform most of the "noneconomical" work, at least in modern Western societies.

Another example where the concept of the economically active population is likely to yield limited results concerns the whole range of illegal or so-called immoral activities such as prostitution, organized crime, and the like, in short mainly those activities that Marx called the *Lumpenproletariat*. Although some censuses such as Italy's in 1931 do include prostitutes as one separate category (but, interestingly enough, in the section of "economically not active persons" together with people who live off real estate or capital), no official labor force statistics, of course, can be expected about organized crime. This is a very fascinating but equally complex subject which can be very important, but its investigation lies beyond the possibilities of this study.

While labor force studies concentrating on females or the urban labor market may find the concept of the economically active population insufficient for their purposes, the concept is not only useful but preferable for a study concerned with the relationship between the industry structure and economic development. The questions addressed here refer exclusively to labor in the context of an institutional labor market which is governed by supply and demand. How does this type of labor become allocated to different industries with economic development? What factors can be related to these differences? This emphasis, again, does in no way imply that economically active labor is the only productive work in society. On the contrary, since no cross-national comparable data are available on all forms of labor, a study of this segment of work can give us some ideas about the redistribution of work in a population, in particular with regard to the sexual division of labor.

National census bureaus have followed two main procedures to identify the economically active population: the concept of the gainful worker and the concept of the labor force. Both concepts will be explained in the following section.

THE GAINFUL WORKER APPROACH

In most countries before World War II, the economically active population is identified through the gainful worker approach. This includes all persons over a certain age (usually ten years of age) who have an occupation or had one from which they derived monetary rewards, or who in some way assist in the process of production. This approach does not differentiate between present and past occupation or industry, because the statistics refer to employed and unemployed combined. A person who was unemployed at the time of enumeration but who had had an occupation before was classified according to that previous occupation. On the other hand, this approach excludes those persons who were unemployed and never had an occupation before, which is primarily the case with many young people who have been in the labor market for only a short time. Thus, the main shortcoming of this approach is the fact that no distinction is made between unemployed and employed and that, in addition, it excludes people who are competing in the labor market.

THE LABOR FORCE APPROACH

After the World Depression in the late 1920s, most countries realized the need to distinguish between employed and unemployed workers in order to obtain data for manpower programs and employment needs. The labor force approach, therefore, discriminates between employed persons, unemployed persons (who seek work), and the armed forces. Evidently, the labor force approach is the superior one because it not only permits a greater differentiation but it also includes all potential workers, regardless of previous work status.

For the investigation of the industry structure, the important segment of the labor force are the employed workers, because the unemployed may enter an industry that is very different from their previous one. Such interindustry shifts are very interesting and are certainly related to the concern of this investigation, but the examination of unemployment in relation to the sectoral transformation of the labor force represents a study in itself. For the purposes of this study, therefore, the analysis is restricted to persons that were employed in the reference period prior to enumeration for those censuses that followed the labor force approach (which is the case with all selected countries after World War II), while the analysis prior to 1945 has to be based on the gainful worker approach. In all cases, the armed forces were excluded from the study, because their employment changes are rather different from those of the civilian labor force. Despite the preference of this study for the employed labor force, it would have been interesting to combine both employed and unemployed persons in order to make the labor force approach more comparable to the gainful worker approach. Unfortunately, however, the unemployed group in the labor force approach usually is not classified by previous industry. Even if they were classified in that way, the reliability of such post-facto classification would leave too much to be desired, particularly when workers are asked to name an industry in which they had worked a long time ago. On the other hand, the differences between the two approaches are not so large as to prevent historical comparisons, particularly with regard to long term trends such as the decline of agricultural employment or the emergence of certain services sectors. They ought to remind us, however, that we should not attribute too much meaning to minor employment changes.

Another difference in the definition of the economically active population, historically as well as cross-nationally, is the lower age limit. In the United States, for example, the gainful worker approach included all persons over ten years of age, while the minimum age of persons in the labor force approach is fourteen (sixteen since 1967). Again, it was decided not to adjust this difference. For one thing, such adjustment is not possible where censuses fail to contain information on the distribution of the labor force by industry and age, and this includes most censuses. Besides this statistical obstacle, an adjustment of age is not even desirable, at least in the context of this investigation.

As economic development progresses, the average educational attainment of the population increases. People remain in school longer and this results, in conjunction with work legislation restricting child labor, in a higher average age of labor market entry. It follows from this that in 1970 the proportion of workers under the age of fourteen is much less than it was in 1920. On the other hand, if a substantial proportion of the population did begin to work after age ten, they do compete in the labor force as much as anyone else and should therefore not be excluded. This point has been observed by McInnis (1971:354) who also argues against adjustment of age: "The rationale here is that the change in the lower age limit should be considered as a matter for analysis, rather than of definition." Studies of changes in the labor force participation rates over time, for example, would have an interest in comparing the economically active population for identical age groups, but the study of the sectoral transformation of the labor force must take all members of the economically active population into consideration. While the refinement of measurement certainly must remain the continuous task of social scientists in order to improve our analyses, a case-by-case decision must be made in regard to the most appropriate level of analysis. Given the concern of this investigation with major historical trends of the labor force and cross-national differences in the industry structure, adjustments such as that of age would likely eliminate important parts of reality through mere definition. On the other hand, the actual differences between the seven selected countries concerning the lower age limit and the way the economically active population is identified are not large enough to invalidate a historical and comparative comparison. The maximum difference in the lower age limit is five years, with the exception of Germany which does not specify a lower age limit. However, given the fact that at least eight years of schooling are mandatory in Germany, no person under thirteen years of age is likely to be in the labor force which is well between the two extreme values of ten and fifteen years.

As far as the difference between the gainful worker approach and the labor force approach is concerned, the German situation can serve as an illustration. Between 1950 and 1961, the German census bureau changed the identification of the economically active population from the gainful worker approach to the labor force approach. A comparison of the differences between these two approaches indicates that they were very small indeed. The conclusion drawn from that comparison was that the differences in the distribution of the labor force between 1950 and 1961 was not a statistical artifact, but that it has to be interpreted as a real change in the industry structure itself (Statistisches Bundesamt, 1967:17). Thus, the change in the identification of the economically active population during the 1920-1970 period does not alter the findings of this study in any substantial way.

REFERENCES

AGGRADI, M.F. (1961) "One hundred years of Italian economy." *Review of the Economic Conditions in Italy* 15 (July): 287-209.

ANDRIEUX, A., and J. LIGNON (1960) *L'ouvrier d'audourd'hui.* Paris.

ARONOWITZ, S. (1973) *False Promises: The Shaping of American Working Class Consciousness.* New York: McGraw-Hill.

ASHWORTH, W. (1960) *An Economic History of England, 1870-1939.* London: Methuen.

BACON, R., and W. ELTIS (1976) *Britain's Economic Problem: Too Few Producers.* London: Macmillan.

BAGWELL, P., and G.E. MINGAY (1970) *Britain and America, 1850-1939: A Study of Economic Change.* London: Routledge and Kegan Paul.

BAIN, J.S. (1966) *International Differences in Industrial Structure.* New Haven, Conn.: Yale University Press.

BAIROCH, P. (1971) "Structure de la population active mondiale de 1700 à 1970." *Annales: Economies, Sociétés, Civilisations* (Paris) 26 (September-October): 960-976.

––– and J. LIMBOR (1968) "Changes in the industrial distribution of the world labour force, by region, 1880-1960." *International Labour Review* 98 (No. 4): 311-336.

BARGER, H. (1951) *The Transportation Industries, 1889-1946: A Study of Output, Employment and Productivity.* New York: National Bureau of Economic Research.

BARKIN, K.D. (1970) *The Controversy over German Industrialization, 1890-1902.* Chicago: The University of Chicago Press.

BAUER, P.T., and B.S. YAMEY (1951) "Economic progress and occupational distribution." *The Economic Journal* 61 (December): 741-755.

BECKWITH, B.P. (1967) *The Next Five Hundred Years,* Jericho, N.Y.: Exposition-University Book.

BELL, D. (1965) *The End of Ideology.* New York: Free Press.

––– (1973) *The Coming of the Post-Industrial Society: A Venture in Social Forecasting.* New York: Basic Books.

––– (1976) *The Cultural Contradictions of Capitalism.* New York: Basic Books.

BENDIX, R., and M.S. LIPSET (1967) *Social Mobility in Industrial Society.* Berkeley: University of California Press.

BETTELHEIM, C. (1947) *Bilan de l'economie Française, 1919-1946.* Paris: Presses Universitaires de France.

BLUM, A.A. (1968) "Computers and clerical workers." Document D 1-68 of the Third International Conference on Rationalization, Automation, and Technological Change, sponsored by the Metal Workers' Union of the Federal Republic of Germany. Oberhausen, Germany.

BRAUDEL, F. (1974) *Capitalism and Material Life, 1400-1800.* New York: Harper and Row.

BRAVERMAN, H. (1974) *Labor and Monopoly Capital: The Degradation of Work in the Twentieth Century.* New York: Monthly Review Press.

BROWNING, H.L. (1972) "Primacy variation in Latin America during the twentieth century." Pp. 55-77 in Actas y Memorias de XXXIX Congreso Internacional de Americanistas, Lima, 1970, Volume 2.

——— (1973) "Some problematics of the tertiarization process in Latin America." Paper prepared for the 40th Congress of Americanists in Rome, Italy, September.

——— and J. SINGELMANN (1978) "The emergence of a service society and its sociological implications." *Politics and Society* 8 (Nos. 3-4).

——— (1975) *The Emergence of a Service Society: Demographic and Sociological Aspects of the Sectoral Transformation of the Labor Force in the U.S.A.* Springfield, VA: National Technical Information Service.

CARDOSO, F.H., and E. FALETTO (1970) *Dependência e Desenvolvimento na América Latina.* Rio de Janeiro: Zahar Editores.

CARDOSO, F.H., and J.L. REYNA (1969) "Industrialization, occupation structure, and social stratification in Latin America." Pp. 19-55 in Cole Blasier (ed.), *Constructive Change in Latin America.* Pittsburgh: University of Pittsburgh Press.

CASTELLS, M. (1978) *American Dreams and Capitalist Nightmares: The Economic Crisis and U.S. Society.* Princeton, N.J.: Princeton University Press.

CAVES, R.E., and R.H. HOLTON (1959) *The Canadian Economy.* Cambridge: Harvard University Press.

CEPAL (Economic Commission for Latin America). (1956) "Changes in employment structure in Latin America, 1945-55." *Economic Bulletin for Latin America* 2 (February): 15-42.

CLAPHAM, J.H. (1936) *The Economic Development of France and Germany, 1815-1914.* Cambridge: The University Press.

CLARK, C. (1940) *The Conditions of Economic Progress.* London: Macmillan.

CLOUGH, S.B. (1946) "Retardative factors in French economic development in the nineteenth and twentieth centuries." *The Journal of Economic History* 6 (Supplement): 91-102.

——— (1964) *The Economic History of Modern Italy.* New York: Columbia University Press.

COCHRAN, T.C., and W. Miller (1961) *The Age of Enterprise: A Social History of Industrial America.* New York: Harper and Row.

COCKROFT, J.D., A.G. FRANK, and D.L. JOHNSON (1972) *Dependence and Underdevelopment: Latin America's Political Economy.* Garden City, N.Y.: Doubleday.

COLE, R.E. (1971) *Japanese Blue Collar.* Berkeley: University of California Press.

——— (1973) "Functional alternatives and economic development: an empirical example of permanent employment in Japan." *American Sociological Review* 38 (August): 424-438.

DAHRENDORF, R. (1959) *Class and Class Conflict in Industrial Society.* Stanford: Stanford University Press.

––– (1967) "Recent changes in the class structure of European societies." Pp. 291-336 in S.R. Graubard (ed.), *A New Europe?* Boston: Beacon.

DAVIS, K. (1969) *World Urbanization 1950-1970. Volume I: Basic Data for Cities, Countries, and Regions.* Population Monograph Series No. 4. Berkeley: Institute of International Studies.

––– and H.H. GOLDEN (1954) "Urbanization and the development of preindustrial areas." *Economic Development and Cultural Change* 3 (October): 6-26.

DENISON, E.F. (assisted by J.-P. POULLIER). (1967) *Why Growth Rates Differ: Postwar Experience in Nine Western Countries.* Washington, D.C.: Brookings Institution.

DEWHURST, J.F. (1955) *America's Needs and Resources: A New Survey.* New York: Twentieth Century Fund.

DILLARD, D. (1967) *Economic Development of the North Atlantic Community.* Englewood Cliffs, N.J.: Prentice Hall.

DORE, R. (1973) *British Factory, Japanese Factory: The Origins of National Diversity in Industrial Relations.* Berkeley: University of California Press.

DUNCAN, O.D. (1959) "Service industries and the urban hierachy." *Regional Science Association* (Proceedings) 5:105-120.

EASTERBROOK, W.T., and H.G.J. AITKEN (1956) *Canadian Economic History.* Toronto: Macmillan.

EMI, K. (1971) "The structure and its movements of the tertiary industry in Japan." *Hitotsubachi Journal of Economics* 12 (June):22-32.

FABRICANT, S. (1952) *The Trend of Government Activity in the United States Since 1900.* New York: National Bureau of Economic Research.

FAUNCE, W.A. (1968) *Problems of an Industrial Society.* New York: McGraw-Hill.

FIRESTONE, O. (1958) *Canada's Economic Development, 1867-1953.* London: Bowes and Bowes.

FIRTH, R. (1948) "Anthropological background to work." *Occupational Psychology* 22:94-102.

FISHER, A.G.B. (1935) *The Clash of Progress and Security.* London: Macmillan.

––– (1952) "A note on tertiary production." *Economic Journal* 62 (Dec.): 820-34.

––– (1954) "Tertiary production: A postscript." *Economic Journal* 64 (Sept.) 619-21.

FISHLOW, A. (1966) *American Railroads and the Transformation of the Antebellum Economy.* Cambridge, Mass.: Harvard University Press.

FOURASTIÉ, J. (1963) *Le Grand Espoir du XXe Siècle.* Paris.

FUCHS, V.R. (1968) *The Service Economy.* New York: National Bureau of Economic Research.

––– (ed.) (1969) *Production and Productivity in the Service Industries: Studies in Income and Wealth Service* No. 34. New York: National Bureau of Economic Research.

GALBRAITH, J.K. (1971) *The New Industrial State.* Boston: Houghton Mifflin.

GARTNER, and L. RIESSMAN (1974) *Service Society and the Consumer Vanguard.* New York: Harper and Row.

GIBBS, J.P., and W.T. MÀRTIN (1958) "Urbanization and natural resources: A study in organizational ecology." *American Sociological Review* 23 (June): 266-277.

GIST, N.P., and S.F. FAVA (1964) *Urban Society.* Fifth Edition. New York: Thomas Y. Crowell.

GOLDSMITH, R.W. (1958) *Financial Intermediaries in the American Economy since 1900.* New York: National Bureau of Economic Research.

GOLDTHORPE, J.H., D. LOCKWOOD, F. BECHOFER, and J. PLATT. (1968) *The Affluent Worker: Industrial Attitudes and Behavior.* Cambridge: The University Press.

GRAF, H.G. (1968) *Der Einfluss des Einkommens auf die Struktur des Dienstleistungssektors.* Zürich and St. Gallen: Polygraphischer Verlag.

GREENFIELD, H.I. (1966) *Manpower and the Growth of Producer Services.* New York: Columbia University Press.

HABAKKUK, H.J. (1955) "The historical experience on the basic conditions of economic progress." Pp. 149-169 in L.H. Dupriez (ed.), *Economic Progress.* Louvain: Institut de Recherches Economiques et Sociales.

HANSON, N.M. (1968) *French Regional Planning.* Bloomington, Indiana: Indiana University Press.

HARDIN, R. (1976) "Stability of statist regimes: industrialization and institutionalization. Pp. 147-168 in T.R. Burns and W. Buckley (eds.), *Power and Control: Social Structures and Their Transformation.* Beverly Hills: Sage Publications.

Harvard University (1969) *Technology and Work.* Harvard University Program on Technology and Society. Research Review No. 2. Cambridge, Mass.

HEILBRONER, R.L. (1976) *Business Civilization in Decline.* New York: W.W. Norton.

HIRSCHMAN, A.O. (1958) *The Strategy of Economic Development.* New Haven, Conn.: Yale University Press.

HOBSBAWM, E.J. (1969) *Industry and Empire.* The Pelican History of Britain, Volume 3. London: Penguin.

––– (1975) The Age of Capital. New York: Scribner's.

HODGETT, G.A.J. (1971) *A Social and Economic History of Medieval Europe.* New York: Harper and Row.

HOFFMANN, W.G. (1965) *Das Wachtum der Deutschen Wirtschaft.* Berlin: Springer.

HOSELITZ, B.F. (1961) "Some quantitative problems in the study of industrialization." *Economic Development and Cultural Change* 9:537-546.

HUBER, B.J. (1971) "Studies of the future: A selected and annotated bibliography." Pp. 339-454 in W. Bell and J.A. Mau (eds.), *The Sociology of the Future.* New York: Russell Sage Foundation.

HULTGREN, T. (1948) *American Transportation in Prosperity and Depression.* New York: National Bureau of Economic Research.

Institut für Arbeitsmarkt- und Berufsforschung (1971) "Neue Messverfahren der Berufsforschung." *Materialien aus der Arbeitsmarkt- und Berufsforschung* No. 28.

JAGUARIBE, H., A. FERRER, M.S. WIONCZEK, and T. DOS SANTOS (1970) *La dependencia político-económica de America Latina.* Mexico City: Siglo Veintiuno Editores.

JANOWITZ, M. (1976) *Social Control of the Welfare State.* New York: Elsevier.

KAHN, H., and A.J. WIENER (1967) "The next thirty-three years: A framework for speculation." *Daedalus* (Summer): 705-732.

KATOUZIAN, M.A. (1970) "The development of the service sectors: A new approach." *Oxford Economic Papers,* 22 (November): 362-82.

KERN, H., and M. SCHUMANN (1970) *Industriearbeit und Arbeiterbewusstsein.* Two parts. Wirtschaftliche und soziale Aspekte des technischen Wandels in der Bundesrepublik Deutschland, Volume 8. Frankfurt am Main: Europäische Verlagsanstalt.

KINDLEBERGER, C.P. (1962) *Foreign Trade and the National Economy*. New Haven, Conn.: Yale University Press.

KUZNETS, S., and W.E. MOORE, and J.J. SPENGLER (eds.) (1955) *Economic Growth: Brazil, India, Japan*. Durham, N.C.: Duke University Press.

KUZNETS, S. (1957) "Quantitative aspects of the economic growth of nations, II: Industrial distribution of national product and labor force." *Economic Development and Cultural Change* 5 (July), Supplement.

――― (1966) *Modern Economic Growth*. New Haven, Conn.: Yale University Press.

――― (1971) *Economic Growth of Nations: Total Output and Production Structure*. Cambridge, Mass.: The Belknap Press of Harvard University Press.

LAMBERT, D. (1965) "L'urbanisation accélérée de l'Amerique Latine et la formation d'un secteur tertiare refuge." *Civilisations* 15 (Nos. 2-4): 158-174, 309-325, 477-492.

LANCE, E.D. et al. (1972) *American Economic Growth: An Economist's History of the United States*. New York: Harper and Row.

LANDES, D.S. (1969) *The Unbound Prometheus: Technological Change and Industrial Development in Western Europe from 1750 to the Present*. Cambridge, Mass.: Cambridge University Press.

LASCH, C. (1972) "Toward a theory of post-industrial society." Pp. 36-50 in M.D. Hancock and G. Sjoberg (eds.), *Politics in the Post-Welfare State*. New York: Columbia University Press.

LEVISON, A. (1974) *The Working Class Majority*. London: Penguin.

LEVITT, T. (1976) "Management and the 'post-industrial' society." *The Public Interest* 44 (Summer): 69-103.

LEWIS, W.A. (1955) *Theory of Economic Growth*. London: Allan and Unwin.

LITHWICK, N. (1967) *Economic growth in Canada*. Toronto: University of Toronto Press.

LOCKWOOD, W.W. (1968) *The Economic Development of Japan*. Expanded edition. Princeton, N.J.: Princeton University Press.

LÜTGE, F.K. (1966) *Deutsche Sozial-und Wirtschaftsgeschichte: Ein Überblick*. Third enlarged edition. Berlin: Springer.

LUTZ, V.C. (1962) *Italy: A Study in Economic Development*. New York: Oxford University Press.

MACHLUP, F. (1962) *The Production and Distribution of Knowledge in the United States*. Princeton, N.J.: Princeton University Press.

MANCHESTER, W. (1970) *The Arms of Krupp–1587-1968*. New York: Bantam.

MALLET, S. (1963) *La Nouvelle Classe Ouvrière*. Paris: Editions du Seuil.

MANDEL, E. (1972) *Der Spätkapitalismus*. Frankfurt/Main: Suhrkamp.

――― (1968) *Marxist Economic Theory*. 2 Vols. New York: Monthly Review Press.

MANSFIELD, E. (1968) *Industrial Research and Technological Innovation*. New York: W.W. Norton.

McINNIS, R.M. (1971) "Long-run changes in the industrial structure of the Canadian work force." *Canadian Journal of Economics* 4 (August): 353-361.

MENZ, L. (1965) *Der Tertiäre Sektor: Der Dienstleistungsbereich in den modernen Volkswirtschaften*. Zürich and St. Gallen: Polygraphischer Verlag.

METHA, S.K. (1961) "A comparative analysis of the industrial structure of the urban labor force of Burma and the United States." *Economic Development and Cultural Change* 9 (January): 164-179.

MYERS, G.C. (1972) "Temporal perspectives in urban ecology." Paper prepared for

Annual Meetings of the Southern Sociological Society, April.

NURKSE, R. (1970) (1953) *Problems of Capital Formation in Underdeveloped Countries.* New York: Oxford University Press.

OGBURN, W.F., and W. JAFFE (1929) *The Economic Development of Post-War France.* New York: Columbia University Press.

OKAWA, K. (1957) *The Growth Rate of the Japanese Economy since 1878.* Tokyo: Kinokuniya Bookstore Co.

OPPENHEIMER, V.K. (1970) *The Female Labor Force in the United States.* Population Monograph Series, No. 5. Berkeley: Institute of International Studies.

OSHIMA, H.T. (1971) "Labor-force 'explosion' and the labor-intensive sector in Asian growth." *Economic Development and Cultural Change* 19 (January): 161-83.

O'TOOLE, J. (1974) *Work and the Purity of Life: Resource Papers for Work in America.* Cambridge, Mass.: MIT Press.

PERROUX, F. (1955) "Prises de vues sur la croissance de l'économie française, 1780-1950." Pp. 41-68 in S. Kuznets (ed.), *Income and Wealth,* Series V. London: Bowes and Bowes.

PETERSON, J.M., and R. GRAY (1969) *Economic Development of the United States.* Homewood, Ill.: Richard D. Irwin.

POSTAN, M.M. (1967) *An Economic History of Western Europe, 1945-1964.* London: Methuen.

––– (1971) *Fact and Relevance: Essays on Historical Method.* Cambridge, England: Cambridge University Press.

PRYOR, F.L. (1973) *Property and Organization in Capitalist and Communist Countries.* Urbana: University of Illinois Press.

RICHTA, R. (1977) "The scientific and technological revolution and the prospects of social development." Pp. 25-72 in *Scientific-Technological Revolution: Social Aspects.* Beverly Hills: Sage Publications.

ROSENSTEIN-RODAN, P.N. (1943) "Problems of industrialization of Eastern and Southeastern Europe." *Economic Journal* (June-September): 204-207.

ROSTOW, W.W. (1960) *The Stages of Economic Growth: A Non-Communist Manifesto.* Cambridge, Mass.: Cambridge University Press.

RUSHER, W. (1975) *The Making of the New Majority Party.* New York: Greenhill.

SABALO, Y. (1971) "A structural approach to the projection of occupational categories and its application to South Korea and Taiwan." *International Labour Review* 103 (February): 131-155.

––– [assisted by J. Gaude and R. Wéry] (1975) *The Service Industries.* Geneva: International Labour Office.

SCHULTZ, T.W. (1964) *Transforming Traditional Agriculture.* New Haven, Conn.: Yale University Press.

SENGUPTA, J.K. (1958) "On the relevance of the sectoral concept in the theory of economic development." *Indian Economic Journal* 6 (July): 50-61.

SINGELMANN, J. (1974) *The Sectoral Transformation of the Labor Force in Seven Industrialized Countries,* 1920-1960. Ph.D. dissertation. Austin: The University of Texas.

––– and E.O. WRIGHT (1978) "Proletarianization in advanced capitalist countries: an empirical intervention into the debate between Marxists and post-industrial theorists over the transformation of the labor process." Presented at the Conference on the Labor Process, SUNY, Binghamton, May 5-7.

SINGER, P. (1971) "Forca de trabalho e emprego no Brasil: 1920-1969." *Cadernos CEBRAP* 3. Sao Paulo: CEBRAP.

SORRENTINO, C. (1971) "Comparing employment shifts in 10 industrialized countries." *Monthly Labor Review* (October): 3-11.

STATISTISCHES BUNDESAMT. (1967) *Volks- und Berufszählung vom 6. Juni 1961.* Heft 12: *Erwerbspersonen in wirtschaftlicher* und *sozialer Gliederung.* Stuttgart: Kohlhammer.

STEINER, F.B. (1957) "Towards a classification of labour." *Sociologus* 7 (No. 2): 112-129.

STONE, L.L. (1967) *Urban Development in Canada.* 1961 Census Monograph. Ottawa: Dominion Bureau of Statistics.

TAEUBER, I.B. (1958) *The Population of Japan.* Princeton, N.J.: Princeton University Press.

— — — and C. TAEUBER (1971) *People of the United States in the 20th Century.* A Census Monograph. Washington, D.C.: U.S. Government Printing Office.

THOMAS, B. (1961) *International Migration and Economic Development: A Trend Report and Bibliography.* Paris: UNESCO.

THOMSON, I.B. (1970) *Modern France: A Social and Economic Geography.* London: Butterworths.

New York Times (1977) "To say productivity is one thing; to measure it is another." March 27.

TOFFLER, A. (1970) *Future Shock.* New York: Random House.

TOURAINE, A. (1971) *The Post-Industrial Society: — Tomorrow's Social History: Classes, Conflicts and Culture in the Programmed Society.* New York: Random House.

— — — (1977) "Science, intellectuals and politics." Pp. 109-130 in *Scientific-Technological Revolution: Social Aspects.* Beverly Hills: Sage Publications.

TRIANTES, S.G. (1953) "Economic progress, occupational redistribution, and international terms of trade." *Economic Journal* 63 (September): 627-637.

TSURUTANI, T. (1976) "Japan as a postindustrial society." Pp. 100-125 in Leon N. Lindberg (ed.), *Politics and the Future of Industrial Society.* New York: David McKay.

United Nations (1958) *International Standard Industry Classification.* New York: United Nations.

Upjohn Institute (1973) *Work in America.* Report of a Special Task Force to the Secretary of Health, Education, and Welfare. Cambridge, Mass.: MIT Press.

U.S. Department of Labor (1973) *New Measures of Labor Force Projection.* A Research Report. Springfield, Va.: Technical Information Service.

WALTER, F. (1957) "Recherches sur le développement économique de la France, 1900-1955." *Cahiers de l'Institut de Science Economique Appliquée,* Series D, No. 9.

WHITE, O., Jr., and G. SJOBERG (1972) "The emerging 'new politics' in America." Pp. 11-35 in M.D. Hancock and G. Sjoberg (eds.), *Politics in the Post-Welfare State.* New York: Columbia University Press.

WILENSKY, H.L. (1975) *The Welfare State and Equality: Structural and Ideological Roots of Public Expenditures.* Berkeley: University of California Press.

WILSON, J.Q., and P. RACHAL (1977) "Can the government regulate itself?" *The Public Interest* 46 (Winter): 3-14.

WOLFE, M. (1955) "The concept of economic sectors." *The Quarterly Journal of Economics* 69 (September): 402-420.

WRIGHT, E.O., and L. PERRONE (1977) "Marxist class categories and income inequality." *American Sociological Review* 42 (February): 32-55.

INDEX

ABOUT THE AUTHOR

JOACHIM SINGELMANN is assistant professor of sociology at Vanderbilt University, Nashville, Tennessee. After studies at the University of Hamburg, Germany and the University of Texas at Austin, he received his Ph.D. from the latter institution in 1974. Dr. Singelmann's research interests have centered around demographic and labor force issues. In addition to a number of articles and papers, he is the author (with Mayer N. Zald and Ivar Berg) of *Occupations and Organizations in American Life* (Belmont, CA.: Wadsworth).